KoKo Bear's New Potty

A Practical Parenting Read-Together Book

Vicki Lansky

Illustrated by Jane Prince

BANTAM BOOKS

TORONTO · NEW YORK · LONDON · SYDNEY · AUCKLAND

KOKO BEAR'S NEW POTTY
A Bantam Book / April 1986
2nd printing January 1987
3rd printing January 1988

Library of Congress Cataloging-in-Publication Data

Lansky, Vicki.
Koko Bear's new potty.

1. Toilet training—Juvenile literature.
I. Title.
HQ770.5.L35   1986   649'.62   85-48233
ISBN 0-553-34243-6 (pbk.)

Published simultaneously in the United States and Canada

Bantam Books are published by Bantam Books, a division of Bantam
Doubleday Dell Publishing Group, Inc. Its trademark, consisting of the
words "Bantam Books" and the portrayal of a rooster, is Registered in
U.S. Patent and Trademark Office and in other countries. Marca
Registrada. Bantam Books, 666 Fifth Avenue, New York, New York
10103.

PRINTED IN THE UNITED STATES OF AMERICA

WAK   12   11   10   9   8   7   6   5   4

Introduction

Toilet training, I believe, is part of an overall urge towards independence and self-reliance that is natural for every child growing up. It is not something you do for children but rather something you help them learn for themselves.

One way you can help is by letting your child understand what to expect and what's expected. With that in mind, the story of KoKo Bear, a loveable little bear, will set an example for your child. KoKo Bear's transition from diapers to independent use of the toilet is a delightful story that you and your child will enjoy reading again and again.

To help you make this a smooth transition, there are tips and suggestions for parents and caregivers on every page. You can skim these silently while you and your child read about KoKo. For more detailed material and additional tips, you may wish to refer to my companion book, Practical Parenting TOILET TRAINING.

Every child is different, therefore readiness for toilet training will be slightly different for each child. Flexibility, gentleness and generous use of praise on your part can make this an easy and pleasant time for both of you.

Please remember, if you find yourself frustrated about your child's progress, that toilet training is a teaching and learning process, not an obedience issue nor a test that must be passed on any set date.

Sincerely,

Vicki Lansky

This is KoKo Bear. KoKo used to be a tiny little bear cub.

Now KoKo is growing up. Doing things for yourself is part of growing up.

What things can you do for yourself? Can you brush your teeth? Can you dress yourself?

- *Praise your child for independent behavior and attempts at self-help.*
- *Discuss with your child the things he or she can already do independently.*
- *Encourage your child's sense of self and control over his or her own world by allowing the extra time it takes to perform these tasks.*

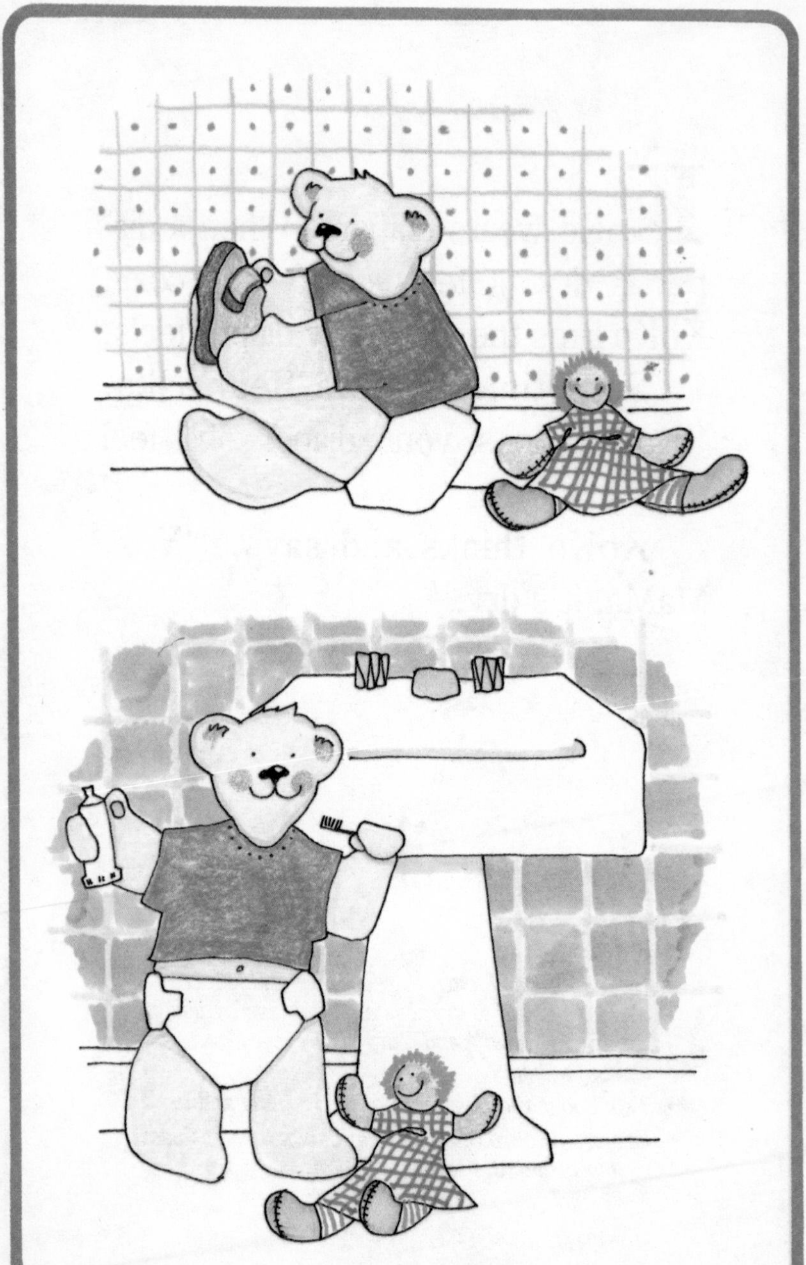

KoKo wears diapers. When a diaper is dry, it feels comfy and cozy. KoKo likes the way a dry diaper feels.

Sometimes MaMa Bear asks, "KoKo, does your diaper still feel dry?"

KoKo thinks and says, "Yes, MaMa, it's dry."

- *Help your child learn to recognize and identify the sensations of dryness and wetness by using the terms "wet" and "dry" whenever you change a diaper.*
- *Talk about the pleasures of being clean and dry.*
- *Change diapers often to help him or her get used to and prefer the feel of a dry diaper.*

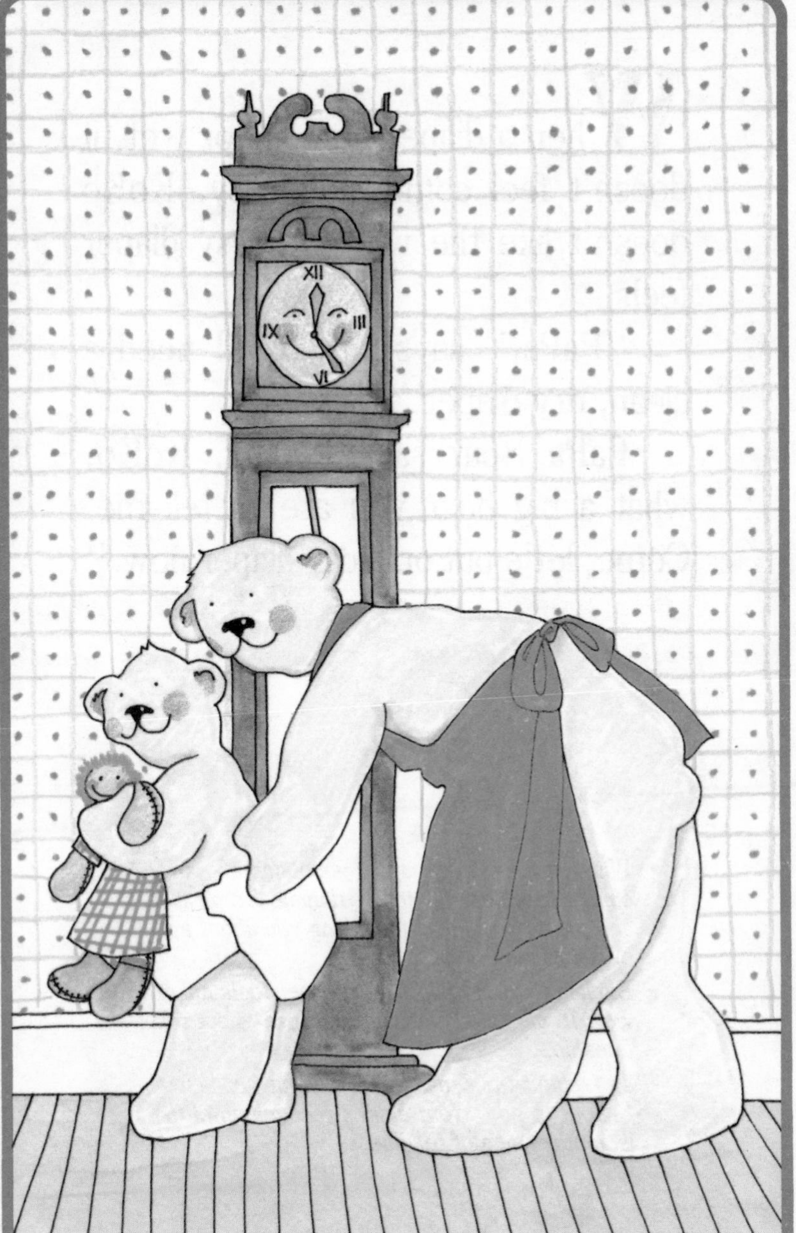

When a diaper gets full or wet, it doesn't feel comfy and cozy. KoKo doesn't like the way a messy diaper feels.

"PaPa," says KoKo, "I need a clean, dry diaper."

PaPa Bear says, "Why, KoKo, what a big bear you are to tell me. Come, let's put on a dry diaper now."

- *Wanting to please you is a good sign of your child's readiness for toilet training. Be pleased and praise your child for telling you about a wet or full diaper.*
- *Explain to your child why a diaper feels full or wet. It will help establish the cause-effect relationship.*
- *Talk about the sensation of "going" or being "about to go." Your child's recognition of these is another sign of readiness.*

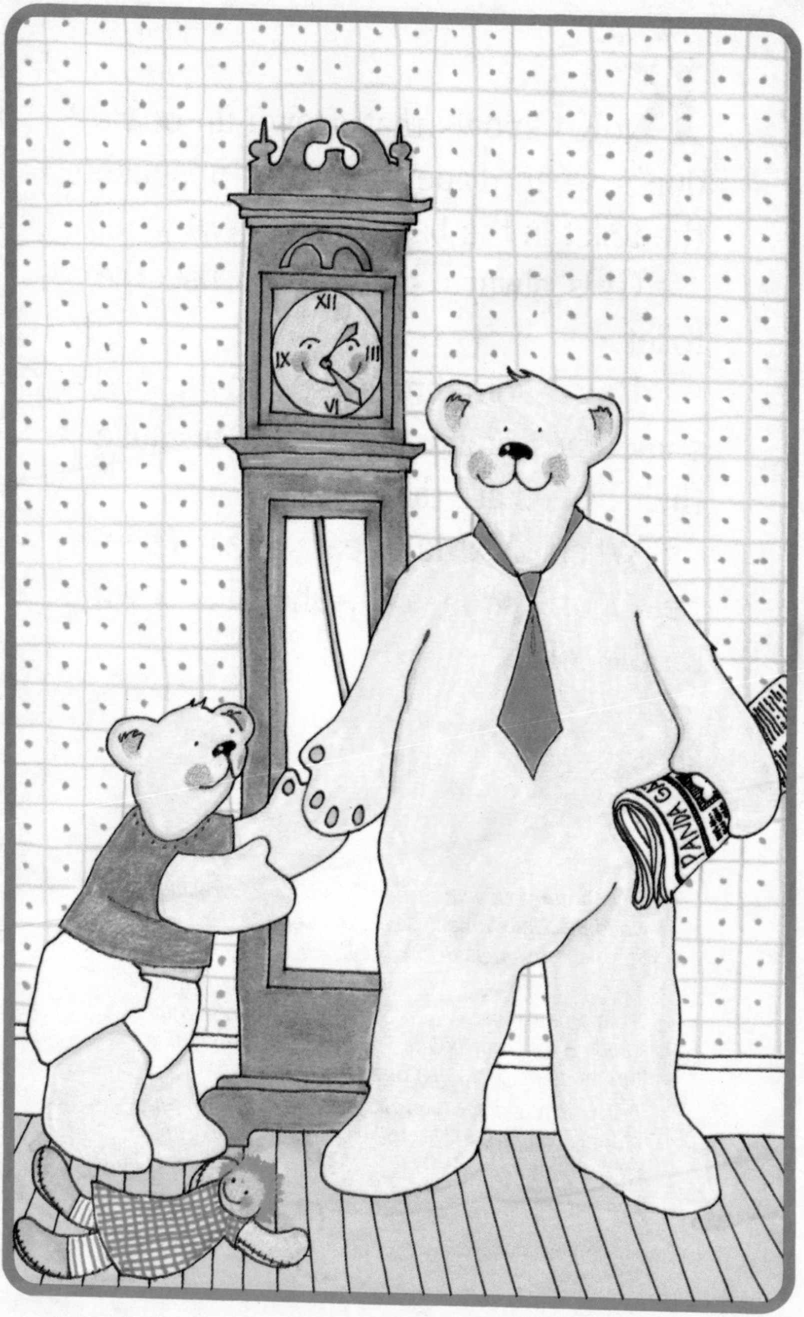
PANDA

KoKo knows that grown-up bears don't wear diapers. Grown-ups use the toilet in the bathroom.

Girls always sit down to use the toilet.

Boys sometimes sit down and sometimes stand up. That's because their bodies are different.

When MaMa Bear goes (*pee-pee**) or (*poo-poo**), she sits down on the toilet.

* *Substitute your familiar family words for urination and bowel movement when you see the parenthesis here and throughout the book.*
* *Decide early—before training begins—which family words to use. Then be consistent with your child. Avoid words like "yucky" that imply body functions or parts are dirty or disgusting.*
* *Let your child see you or others—a parent, an older sibling—use the toilet at home. Children learn by imitating.*

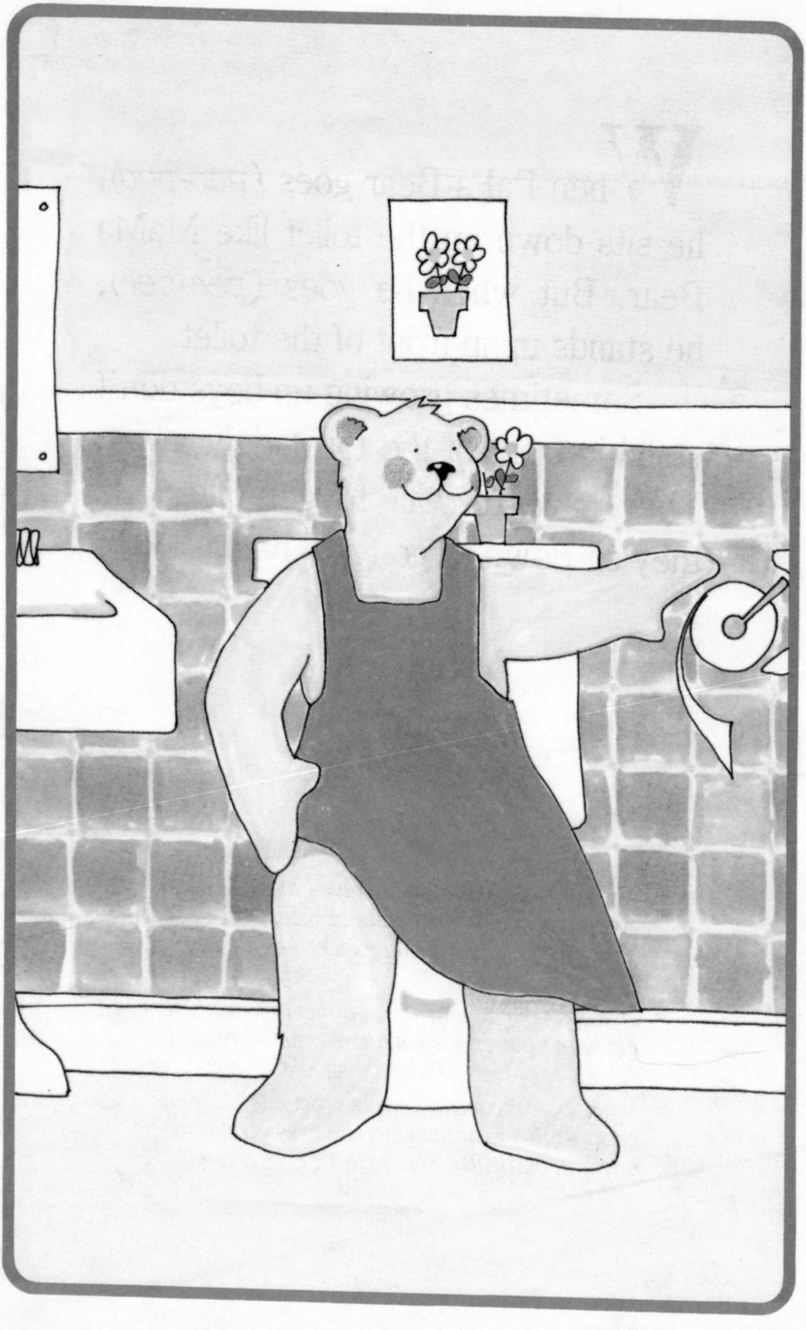

When PaPa Bear goes (*poo-poo*), he sits down on the toilet like MaMa Bear. But when he goes (*pee-pee*), he stands up in front of the toilet.

Sometimes growing-up boys don't stand in front of the toilet right away. They have to wait to get taller. So they sit down to go (*pee-pee*).

- *Going to the bathroom involves many separate acts—from removing pants to using toilet paper. Tell your child what you expect—don't assume he or she knows.*
- *Discuss your timing and approach to toilet training with your spouse and any other caregivers. All adults close to the child should be consistent.*
- *While bowel control usually proceeds bladder control, this is not always the case. Often for boys, in particular, this pattern is reversed.*

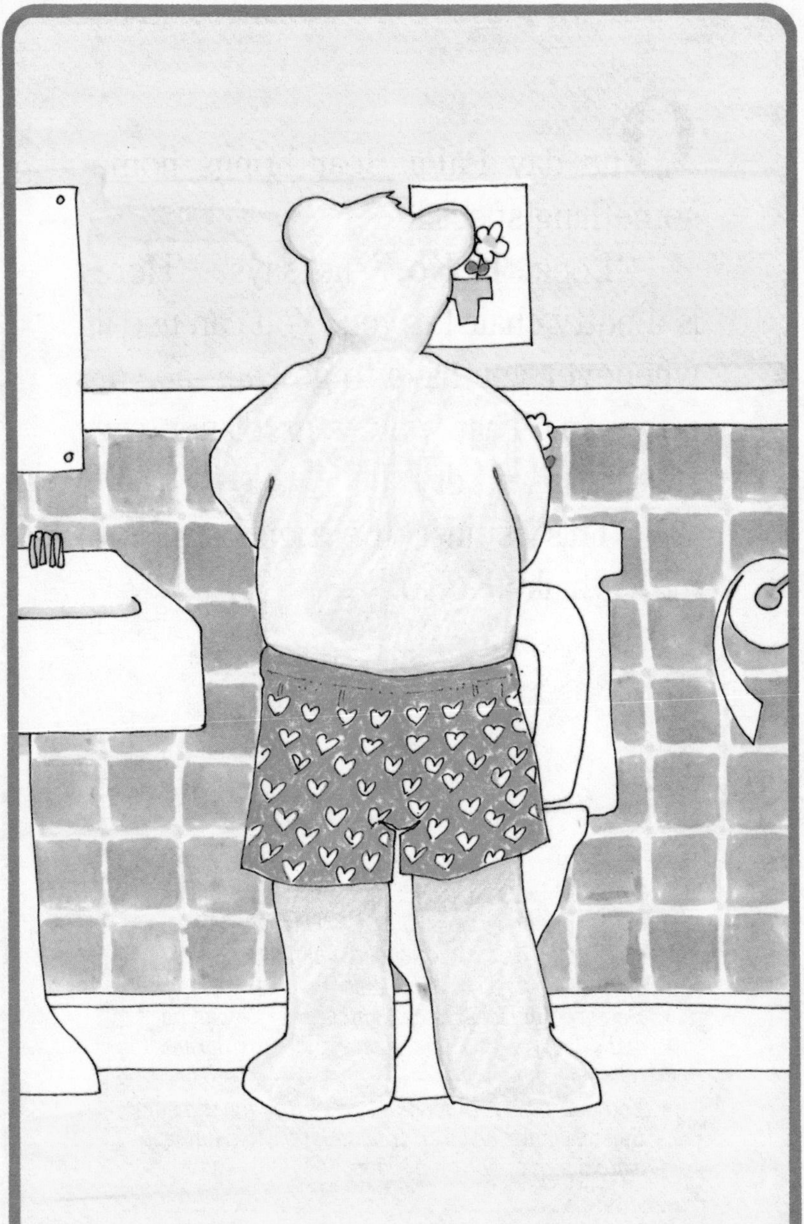

One day PaPa Bear brings home something special.

"Look, KoKo," he says. "Here is a potty chair for you. You can use it whenever you have to go (*pee-pee* or *poo-poo*). That way your diaper can stay clean and dry."

"This is just the right size for me," thinks KoKo.

- *Let your child "practice" sitting on the potty chair with or without clothes. This will help a child feel familiar and comfortable with this new addition.*
- *Be sure your child's clothing is easy to pull on and off. Avoid buttons, snaps and belts during this period.*
- *You don't have to have a potty chair for training. Especially for children trained later, this intermediate aid may not be needed.*

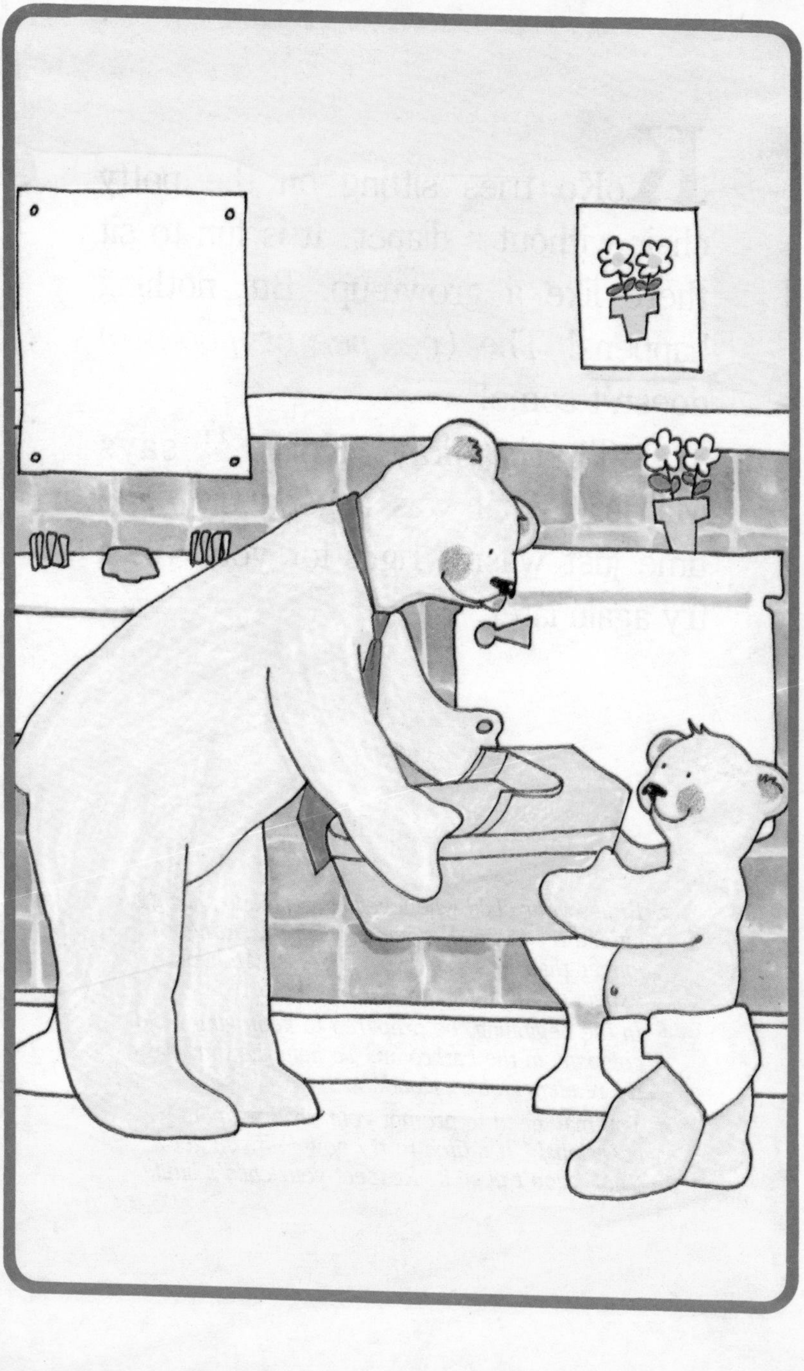

KoKo tries sitting on the potty chair without a diaper. It is fun to sit there like a grown-up. But nothing happens! The (*pee-pee* or *poo-poo*) doesn't come!

"That's okay, KoKo," says MaMa. "That was a good try. The time just wasn't right for you. We'll try again later."

- *Praise your child whenever he or she is willing to sit and try to go. For some children, sitting for longer than 10 seconds is progress! And don't expect a "performance" every time.*
- *In the beginning, be prepared to keep your child company in the bathroom. To help the time pass, try reading a story aloud.*
- *You may need to prompt your child with an occasional "It's time to try now." If you get a "no!" don't push it. Respect your child's limits.*

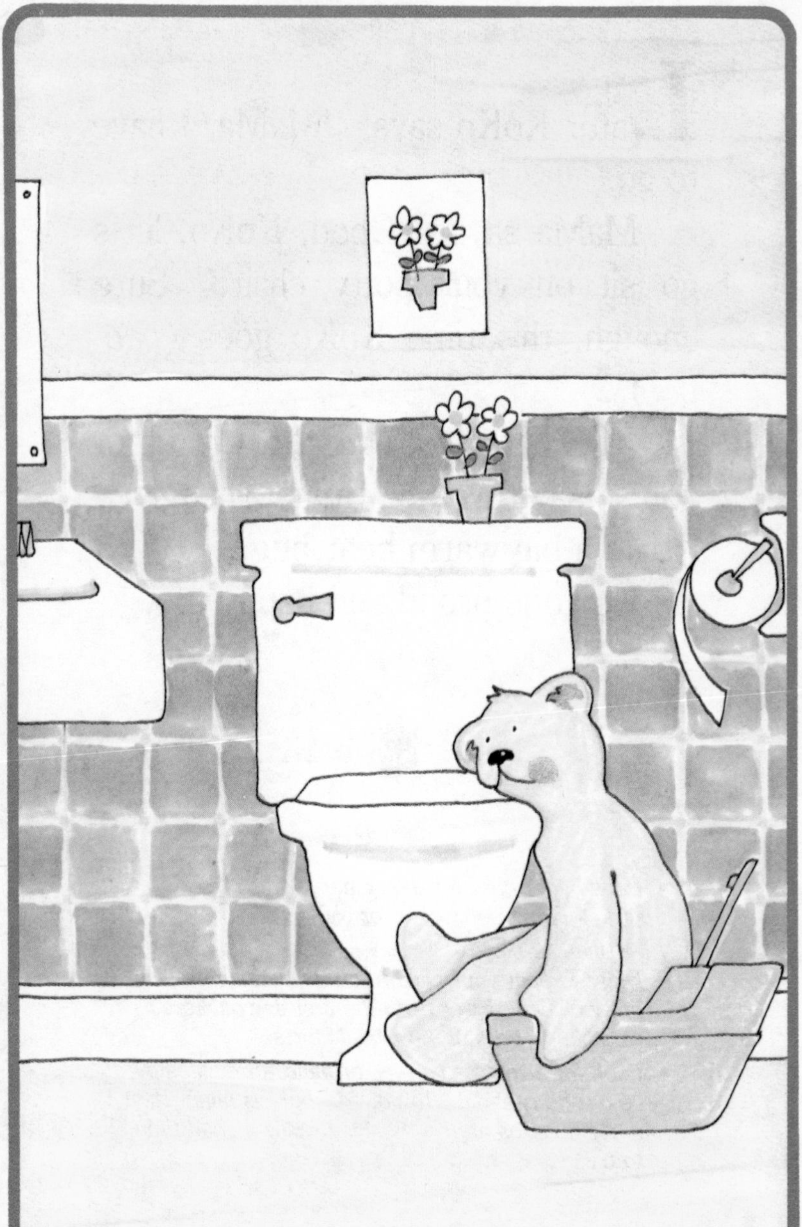

Later KoKo says, "MaMa, I have to go."

MaMa says, "Good, KoKo, let's go sit on your potty chair." Sure enough, this time KoKo goes (*pee-pee*).

"Oh, KoKo, I'm SO proud of you," says MaMa Bear. She gives KoKo a big warm bear hug.

KoKo is proud and happy too.

- *Praise your child for every deposit he or she makes in the potty chair or toilet during this early learning stage.*
- *Don't expect your child to do everything in the potty chair or toilet from the first day on. It is a variable process of stops and starts.*
- *Look for a regular pattern or indicator suggesting he or she is about "to go." If there is none, then thirty minutes after a meal is usually a good time to try.*

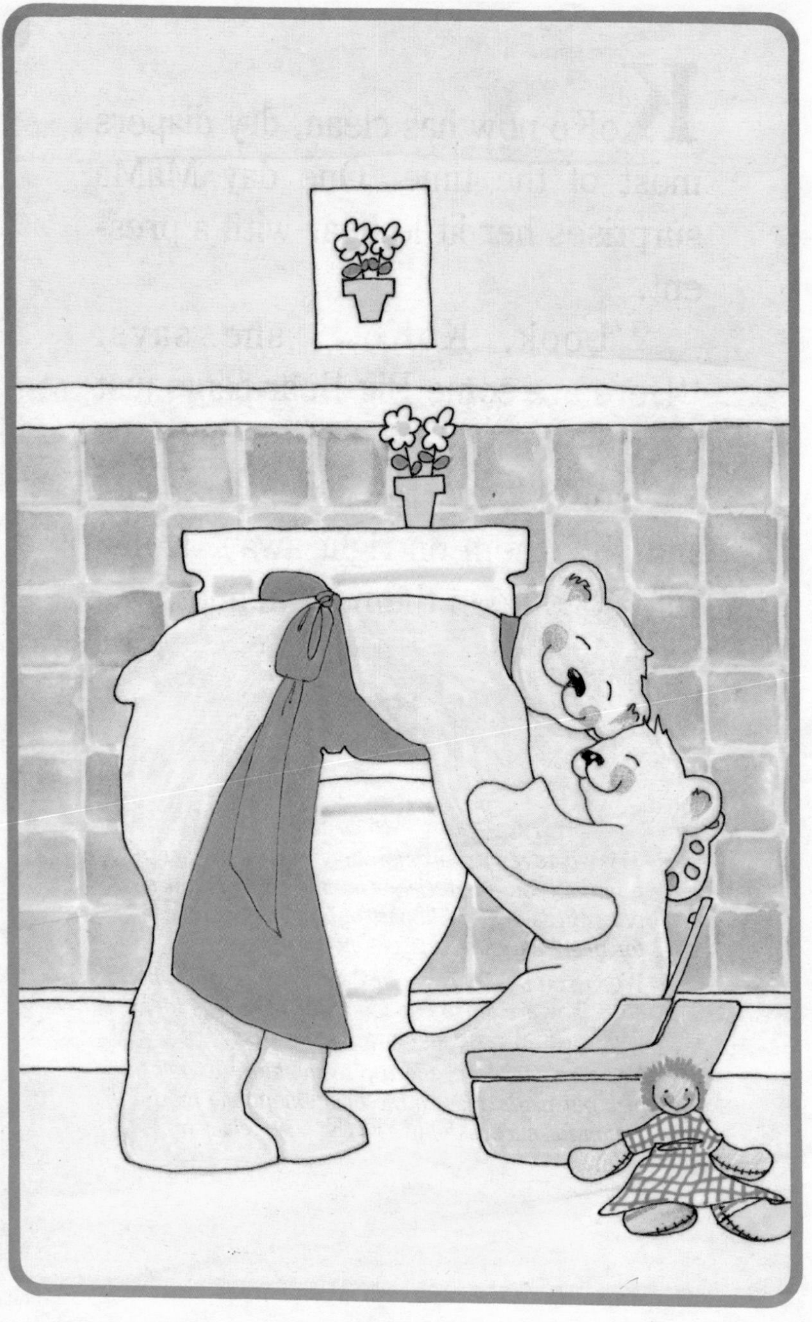

KoKo now has clean, dry diapers most of the time. One day MaMa surprises her little bear with a present.

"Look, KoKo," she says. "Here are some Big-Bear pants just for you."

KoKo loves the Big-Bear pants and puts them on right away. KoKo will try to keep them clean and dry.

- *Try whatever rewards or incentives seem appropriate to you—material or nonmaterial. The use of rewards is a viable part of the training process for many parents and does not last forever.*
- *When you buy "grown-up" or training pants, be sure they are loose enough around the legs for your child to raise and lower them easily.*
- *For some children, the trip to the store to help pick out pants adds to the excitement and motivation for successful use of the potty chair or toilet.*

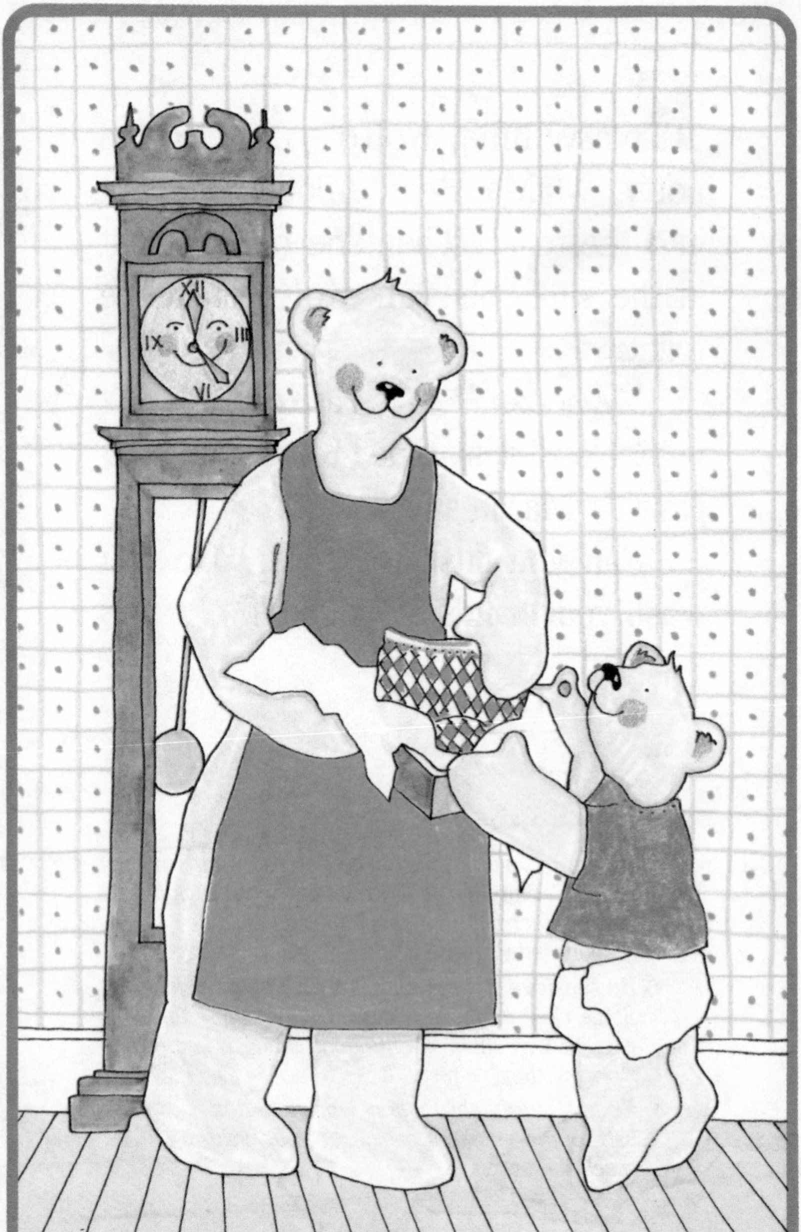
XII
IX
III
VI

Every time KoKo goes to the potty, MaMa Bear empties the pot into the toilet. Then she rinses it out in the sink. She lets KoKo flush the toilet.

"Whoosh," says KoKo.

"Now it's time to wash your paws," MaMa says.

Can you flush the toilet? Do you wash your hands by yourself?

- *It's up to you to decide whether you want your child to empty his or her own potty chair. Some parents feel that this should be the child's responsibility; some don't.*
- *Be sensitive to your child's fears about flushing. Some children find the noise frightening. Others wonder why their parents don't want to keep the "prize" they've just left!*
- *Keep a sturdy child's bench or step-stool in the bathroom to make it easier for your child to reach the sink.*

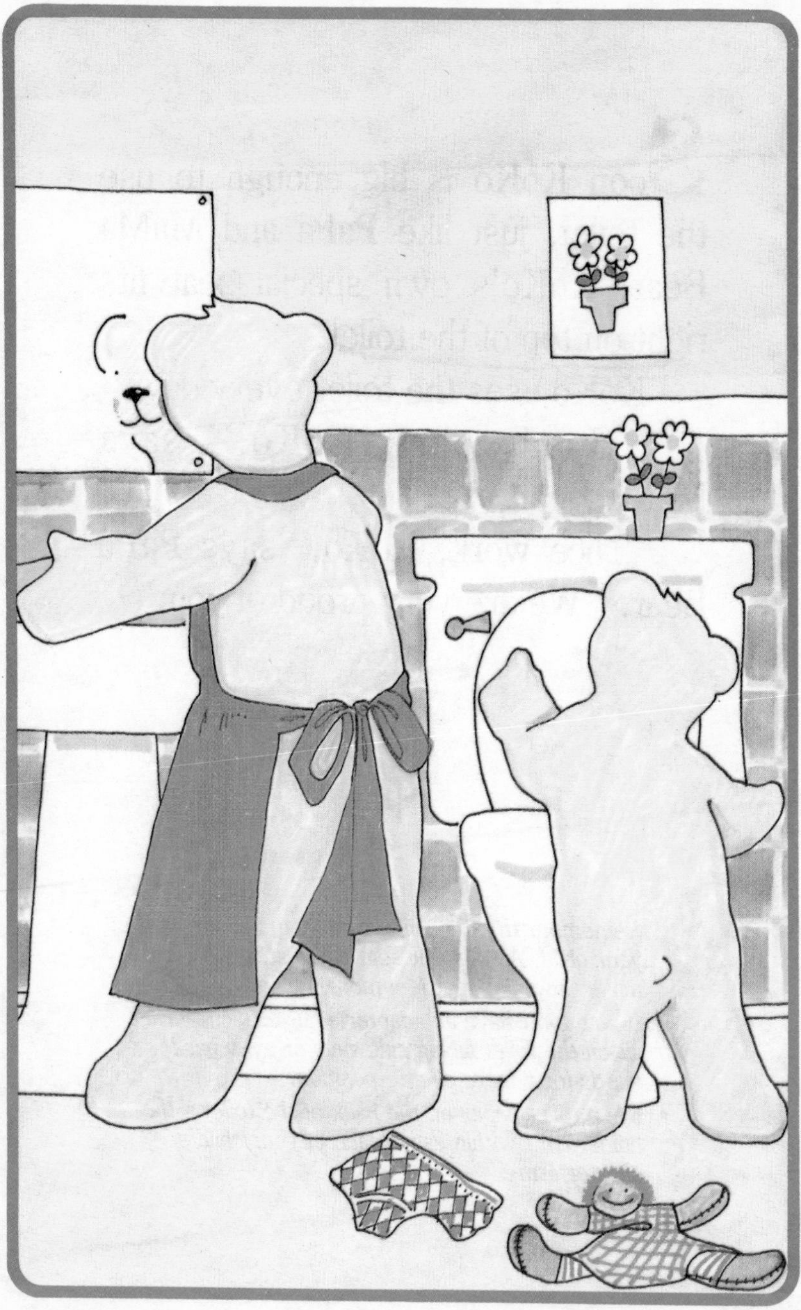

Soon KoKo is big enough to use the toilet, just like PaPa and MaMa Bear. KoKo's own special seat fits right on top of the toilet.

KoKo uses the toilet every day.

"Good going, KoKo," says MaMa Bear.

"Nice work, KoKo," says PaPa Bear. "We are very proud of you."

- *Remember that the toilet can seem awfully big to your child. An adapter seat and a step-stool can make the toilet seat feel more secure.*
- *If you don't have an adapter seat, let your child sit on the toilet facing sideways or even backwards for a more secure position.*
- *Keep toilet paper on the back of the toilet if the holder isn't within easy reach of your child's shorter arms.*

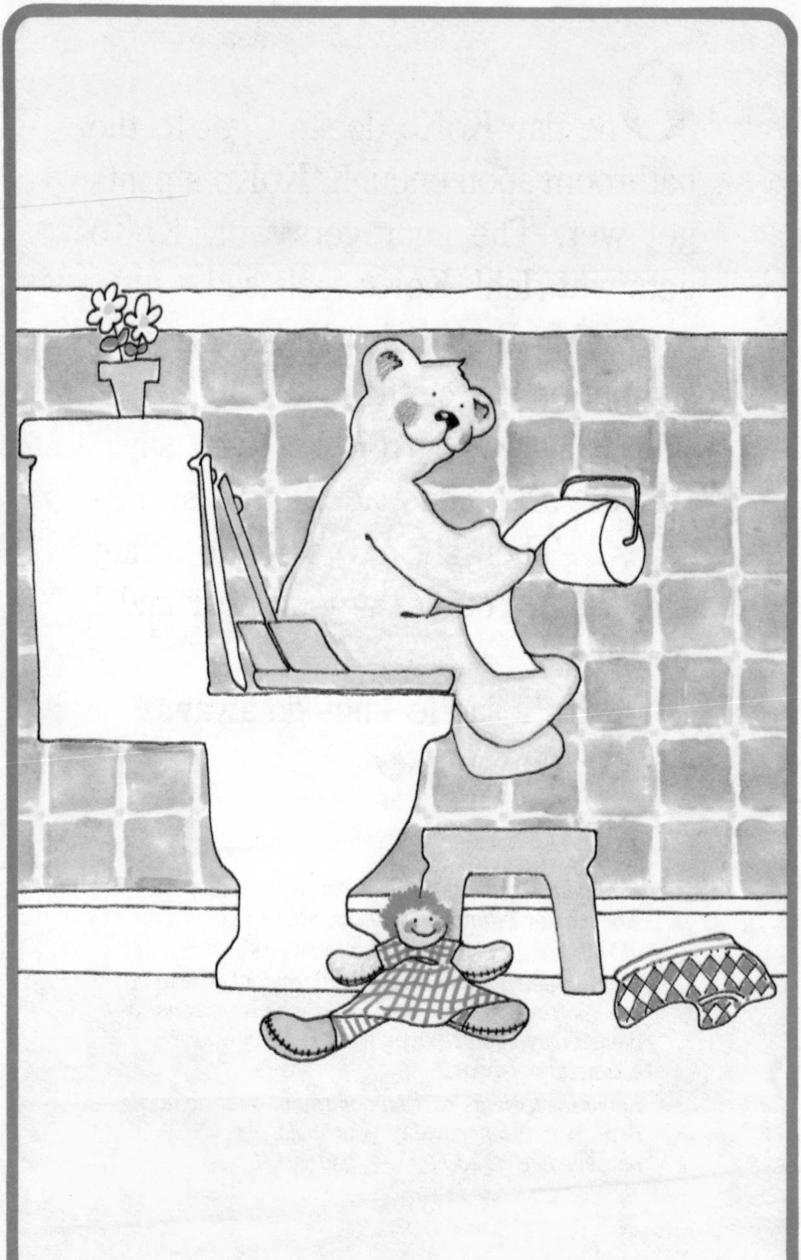

One day KoKo doesn't get to the bathroom soon enough. KoKo's pants get wet. The floor gets wet. KoKo gets wet. Ish! KoKo feels sad.

MaMa Bear helps KoKo clean up and put on dry clothes.

"It's okay, KoKo," she says. "Everybody has accidents sometimes." Then she gives KoKo a hug and kiss. "You are a good bear and I love you."

KoKo's sad feelings go away.

- *Frequent accidents may be caused by allergies, illnesses or other physical conditions. Consider having your child checked by a doctor.*
- *Never punish your child for an accident. Clean up in a matter-of-fact way. A child who is anxious to please may agonize over what is perceived as shameful behavior.*
- *Separate feelings of disappointment over an accident from disapproval of your child. Avoid phrases like "bad boy"—"bad girl."*

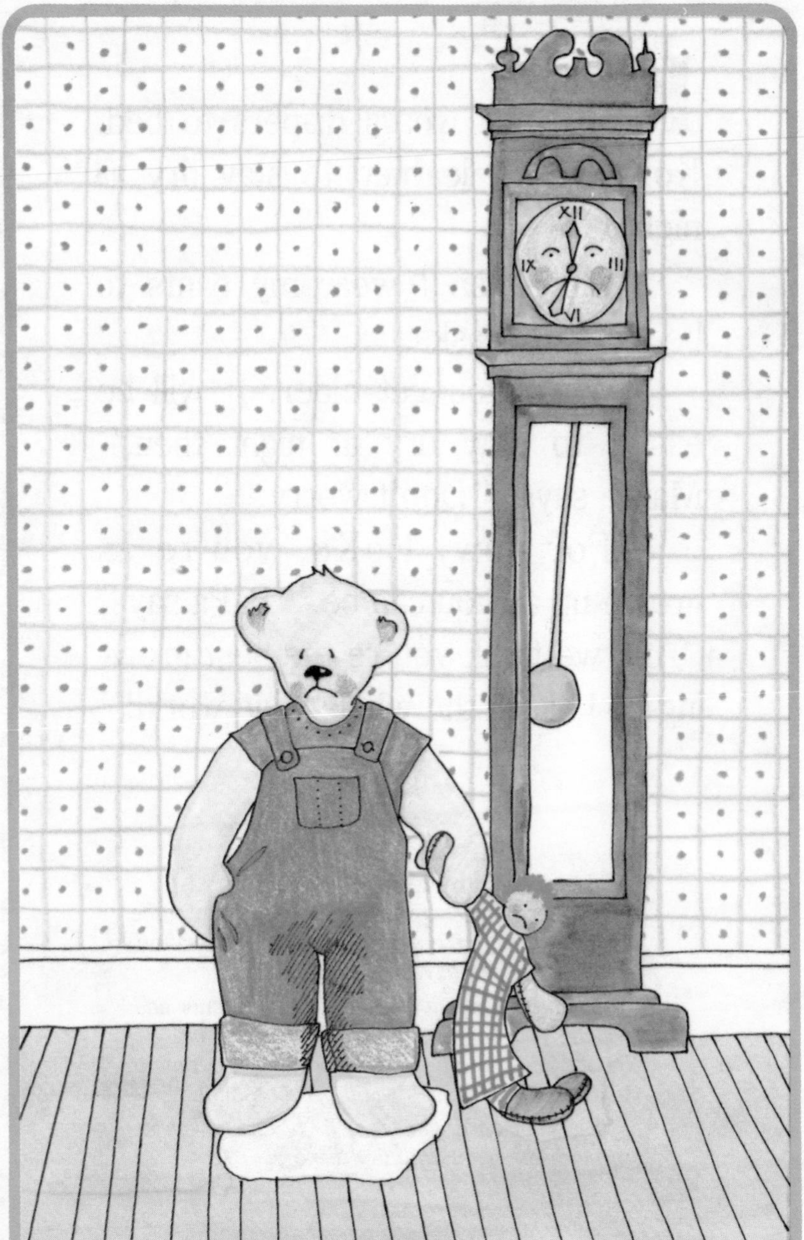
XII
IX
III
VI

KoKo still wears diapers to bed. KoKo hasn't learned to stay dry all night.

"When can I wear my pants to bed?" KoKo asks.

"When you get older. It will be easier to stay dry at night then," MaMa says. "Don't worry."

"For now, KoKo, you're as grown-up as you can be," PaPa says. "And we think you're the best growing-up bear in the whole wide world!"

- *Night-time control requires children to master involuntary muscles while they sleep. For some children it can take months or even years after they've learned daytime control.*
- *You can try limiting fluid intake after dinner and waking your child for a trip to the bathroom before you go to bed, but there is no guarantee that these techniques will be successful.*
- *Praise your child whenever he or she makes it through the night with dry diapers.*

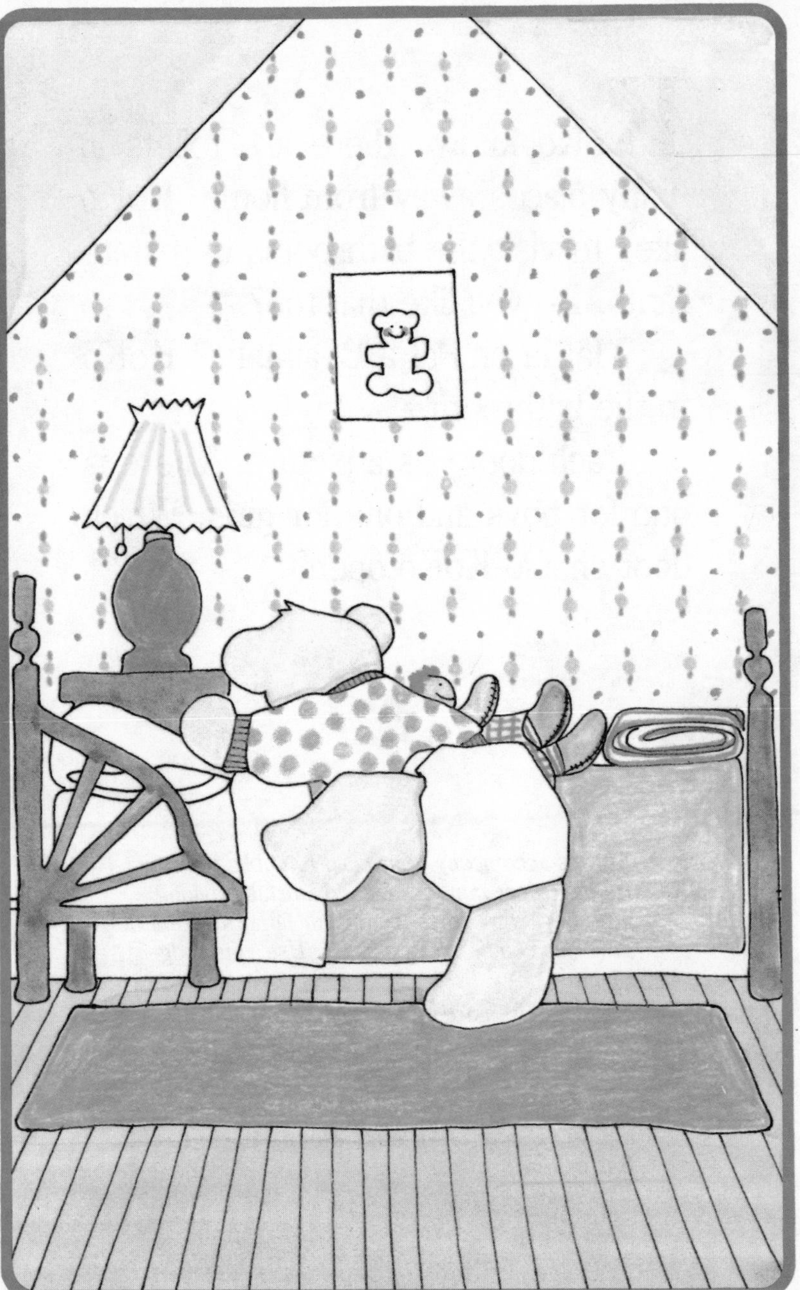

KoKo knows there are toilets in many places away from home. KoKo likes to visit the bathrooms in restaurants. Do you like that too?

MaMa or PaPa Bear takes KoKo to the bathroom.

Each door has a picture. There is one for boys and one for girls. Which door should KoKo open?

- *Always accompany your child to public restrooms. Most mothers feel comfortable taking little boys into ladies' room; for fathers with little girls this can be more difficult. Use your judgment.*
- *Some children are afraid to use strange bathrooms. Respect their fears. This stage passes quickly, as most stages do.*
- *Remember that there are three things you cannot do for your child: **eat—sleep—or go to the bathroom!***

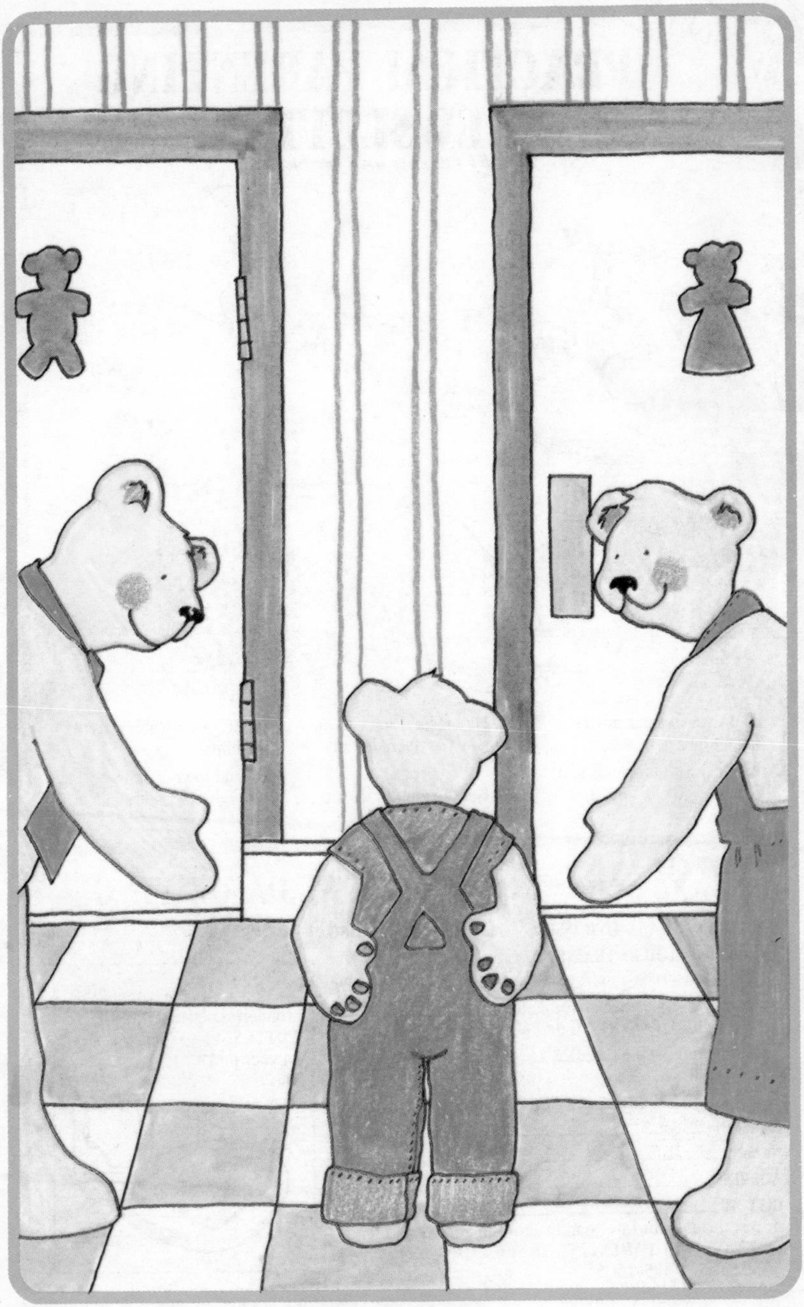

THE GREEK ISLANDS
Genius Loci

View of Naxos island seen through the monumental doorway of the Archaic temple.
Thomas Hope (1769-1831)   Watercolour, 44 x 29 cm.   Benaki Museum, Inv. No. 27375.
© 2010 Benaki Museum, Athens.

Author's acknowledgements

This series of twenty books covering the Aegean Islands is the fruit of many years of solitary dedication to a job difficult to accomplish given the extent of the subject matter and the geography involved. My belief throughout has been that only what is seen with the eyes can trustfully be written about; and to that end I have attempted to walk, ride, drive, climb, sail and swim these Islands in order to inspect everything talked about here. There will be errors in this text inevitably for which, although working in good faith, I alone am responsible. Notwithstanding, I am confident that these are the best, most clearly explanatory and most comprehensive artistic accounts currently available of this vibrant and historically dense corner of the Mediterranean.

Professor Robin Barber, author of the last, general, *Blue Guide to Greece* (based in turn on Stuart Rossiter's masterful text of the 1960s), has been very generous with support and help; and I am also particularly indebted to Charles Arnold for meticulously researched factual data on the Islands and for his support throughout this project. I could not have asked for a more saintly and helpful editor, corrector and indexer than Judy Tither. Efi Stathopoulou, Peter Cocconi, Marc René de Montalembert, Valentina Ivancich, William Forrester and Geoffrey Cox have all given invaluable help; and I owe a large debt of gratitude to John and Jay Rendall for serial hospitality and encouragement. For companionship on many journeys, I would like to thank a number of dear friends: Graziella Seferiades, Ivan Tabares, Matthew Kidd, Martin Leon, my group of Louisianan friends, and my brother Iain— all of whose different reactions to and passions for Greece have been a constant inspiration.

This work is dedicated with admiration and deep affection to Ivan de Jesus Tabares-Valencia who, though a native of the distant Andes mountains, from the start understood the profound spiritual appeal of the Aegean world.

McGILCHRIST'S GREEK ISLANDS

NORTHERN CYCLADES

ANDROS, TINOS &

SYROS

GENIUS LOCI PUBLICATIONS

London

McGilchrist's Greek Islands 18. Northern Cyclades
First edition

Published by Genius Loci Publications
54 Eccleston Road, London W13 0RL

Nigel McGilchrist © 2010
Nigel McGilchrist has asserted his moral rights.

ISBN 978-1-907859–12-0

A CIP catalogue record of this book is available from the British Library.

The author and publisher cannot accept responsibility or liability for
information contained herein, this being in some cases difficult to verify
and subject to change.

Layout and copy-editing by Judy Tither

Cover design by Kate Buckle

Maps and plans by Nick Hill Design

Printed and bound in Great Britain by TJ International Ltd, Padstow, Cornwall

The island maps in this series are based on the cartography of
Terrain Maps
Karneadou 4, 106 75 Athens, Greece
T: +30 210 609 5759, Fx: +30 210 609 5859
terrain@terrainmaps.gr
www.terrainmaps.gr

This book is one of twenty which comprise the complete, detailed
manuscript which the author prepared for the *Blue Guide: Greece,
the Aegean Islands* (2010), and on which the *Blue Guide* was
based. Some of this text therefore appears in the *Blue Guide*.

A NOTE ON THE TEXT & MAPS

Some items in the text are marked with an asterisk: these may be monuments, landscapes, curiosities or individual artefacts and works of art. The asterisk is not simply an indication of the renown of a particular place or item, but is intended to draw the reader's attention to things that have a uniquely interesting quality or are of particular beauty.

A small number of hotels and eateries are also marked with asterisks in the *Practical Information* sections, implying that their quality or their setting is notably special. These books do not set out to be guides to lodging and eating in the Islands, and our recommendations here are just an attempt to help with a few suggestions for places that have been selected with an eye to simplicity and unpretentiousness. We believe they may be the kind of places that a reader of this book would be seeking and would enjoy.

On the island maps:

∴   denotes a site with visible prehistoric or ancient remains

✝   denotes a church referred to in the text
      (on Island Maps only rural churches are marked)

✝   denotes a monastery, convent or large church referred to in the text

⊞   denotes a Byzantine or Mediaeval castle

♟   denotes an ancient stone tower

♨   denotes an important fresh-water or geothermic spring

⛴   denotes a harbour with connecting ferry services

Road and path networks:

-     a continuous line denotes a metalled road
  or unsurfaced track feasible for motors

-     a dotted line denotes footpath only

CONTENTS

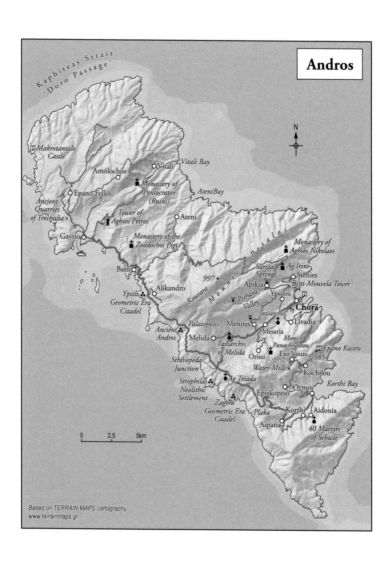

Andros

Kaphireas Strait
'Doro Passage'

Makrotantalo
Castle

Amólochos

Vitali
Vitali Bay

Monastery of
Pontocrator
(Ruins)

AteniBay

Epano Fellos

Ancient
Quarries
of Trochalia

Tower of
Aghios Pétros

Ateni

Gavrio

Monastery of the
Zoodochos Pigi

N

Monastery of
Aghios Nikolaos

Batsi

997

Sariza
Spring

Ag Irini

Ypsili
Geometric Era
Citadel

Alikandro

Kouvara

Apikia

Stenies

Briti-Mouvela Tower

Pithara
Valley

Ypsilou

Chora

Ancient
Andros

Palaiopolis

Menites

Taxiarchis

Livadia

Melida

Mesaria

Moni
Panachrantou

Taxiarchis
of Melida

Orinó

Exo Vouni

Epano Kastro
585

Stravopeda
Junction

Water Mills

Kochilou

Strophilas
Neolithic
Settlement

Ag Triada

Ormos

Korthi Bay

Zagora
Geometric Era
Citadel

Episkopeio

Plaka

Korthi

Aidonia

Aipatia

40 Martyrs
of Sebaste

0   2.5   5km

Based on TERRAIN MAPS cartography
www.terrainmaps.gr

ANDROS

Andros is the second largest island in the Cyclades. It is only marginally smaller than Naxos, but with little over half its population. For this reason its beautiful and varied landscape gives an unexpected sense of spaciousness. The island strikes the visitor immediately as a quiet, reserved, clean and prosperous corner of Greece, well-treed and with water—good water—everywhere. Few other islands can offer such a wealth of shady walks, along valleys of running streams, amongst the flora, bird- and butterfly-life which they support.

The island has given birth to some of the great shipping families of Greece, and this in turn has brought wealth to the island. Notwithstanding its beauty and prosperity, though, it has sought deliberately not to attract tourism. The island is hospitable and provides for everything that the visitor might need; but the infrastructure for mass tourism is thankfully absent here. This is above all a place for the rambler, the cultural tourist and those interested in visiting an island for its peacefulness, normality and unspoiled landscapes.

Andros also offers a number of remarkable museums (including a fine collection of modern Greek art); it has

much archaeological interest, varied landscapes, and an
architecture peculiarly its own. No visit should miss the
well-preserved ancient tower at Aghios Petros; the small
and beautifully clear archaeological museums at Palaiopolis and in Andros Chora; the picturesque villages of
the interior, such as Stenies and Menites; the monastery
of Panachrantos with its iconostasis revetted in 16th century Iznik tiles; the panoramic site of the castle at Apano
Kastro; and a tasting of the waters of the Sariza spring.
All the main archaeological sites run down the western
coast of the island; Andros town or 'Chora', on the other
hand, is on the east coast; and the two deep valleys that
join west and east coasts—the Mesariá valley and, further south, the Korthi valley—are rich in villages, springs
and churches. The north of the island is of a wild and
open spaciousness, and looks onto the stormy Kaphireas
Straits which separate Andros from Euboea and channel
the winds of the open Aegean onto the coasts of Attica—
at times with fabled ferocity.

HISTORY & LEGEND

The island is said to take its name from Andreus, a general of Rhadamanthos of Crete who, according to Diodorus Siculus (V, 79), gifted the island to him; but Pliny records other names—'*Epagris*' or '*Nonagria*'—(*Nat. Hist.* IV, 22); while poets have often simply called the island 'Hydrousa' ('well-watered'). There is good archaeological evidence for prehistoric habitation from the early 3rd millennium onwards, and some for Late Bronze Age settlement. Andros was colonised by Ionians around 900 BC, and the island's most significant early settlements are of the Geometric Period, at Zagorá and Ypsilí.

In the 7th century BC century the city of *Andros* was established and flourished at the west coast site, now called Palaiopolis; in this period the city founded three colonies in Chalcidice, amongst them Stagira, the birth-place of Aristotle. *Andros* had little choice but to join the Persian fleet of Xerxes at Salamis in 480 BC; for this action Themistocles attempted to impose on the islanders a heavy tribute as punishment; on their refusal to pay, he laid siege unsuccessfully to their city (Herodotus, VIII, 108–12). But, in 450 BC the island finally became subject to Athens; and in the 3rd century BC, to Macedon. In 199 BC, the Romans captured it and handed it over to Attalus I of Pergamon: the island then passed back to Rome in the will of Attalus III, together with the rest of his kingdom, and became part of the Roman province of Asia.

In the 9th century, the scholar and logician, Leo the Mathematician, studied on Andros. Notwithstanding devastating raids at the hands of Arabs (8th century), Venetians (12th century), Genoese (15th century), Turks (15th and 16th centuries), and of pirates throughout the whole period, the island appeared prosperous and well-populated, according to the accounts of two 12th century travellers (the Englishman Seawulf, and the Arab Al Idrisi), who comment on the strength of its silk production and trade. In 1207 Marco Sanudo took the island and gave it to the Dandolo family to hold as a hereditary fief under Venice. In 1537 Khaireddin Barbarossa sacked Andros, and—three decades later—in 1566, the island passed officially to the Turks.

Under Ottoman rule it enjoyed a privileged degree of autonomy. Further privileges were accorded to the islanders in 1779 when, after the First Russo-Turkish War, both Syros and Andros were given by Sultan Abdul Hamid I to his favourite niece, Sah Sultana. The freedom and autonomy the two islands subsequently enjoyed allowed them to build merchant fleets and to increase their importance as maritime commercial centres. The island became part of the newly constituted Greek state in 1833, and much of the expansion of the island's commercial fleet took place in the decades immediately following liberation: Andriot ship-owners invested considerably in steam-shipping in the early 20th century. The *National Transoceanic Steamship Line* was registered in Andros, and was the first to operate a service from Greece to New York. In 1927, 79 steamships were registered in Chora. The island's wealth today is owed to the legacy of this intense marine commercial activity.

The guide to the island has been divided into four sections:
- *Andros Chora*
- *Central Andros*
- *The south of the island*
- *The north of the island*

ANDROS CHORA

Arriving by the main road from the west of the island gives little sense of the setting of the Chora. To understand its site it is necessary to approach from either of the two roads which descend the hillsides to north and south: from here the town stretches out below along a needle-like promontory which divides the wide bay into two. The old white-washed town (Kato Kastro) occupies the promontory projecting out into the sea, with the 13th century Venetian fort at its northeastern extremity; the 19th and 20th century town (Ano Chora) fills the area inland and behind. Andros's Chora has none of those reassuring views towards other islands which were so important to the ancient Greeks; it is also exposed to the northerly winds. Perhaps for these reasons there was no settlement here in Antiquity. Later dwellers, who had different needs of defence and transportation, different trade interests and boat designs, subsequently moved here from the old capital on the west coast of the island for the greater protection it offered from piracy, as well as for its greater proximity to the main Aegean trade routes. The settlement of Chora dates from the early 13th century.

Above all, it is the clean lines and spacious dignity of the neoclassical buildings and layout of the town which first strike the visitor today, reflecting the island's shipping-based prosperity during the 19th and early 20th centuries. As a consequence the town is clear and open, but possesses few intimate spaces. At the head of **Embirikou Street,** the main axial artery of Chora, is a recently restored mansion built in 1917 (with remains of a number of the original murals inside), formerly a cultural and electoral centre for the municipality of Andros. This is the town's last and most ostentatious essay in neoclassical design; but the street which it dominates, now mostly closed to traffic and paved with marble, contains many simpler and equally beautiful examples of the same style—such as the hospital at the beginning of the street's south side. The town forms a long thin corridor following the line of this axial street until it reaches the Venetian fort at the sea.

Further on towards the centre and to the right above a small garden, is the church of the Dormition of the Virgin, which has interesting carved capitals in its west portico. Shortly beyond on the same side is a rare example of a pure and unchanged *kafeneion*. Its simple, unadorned interior—spare, clear and understated—contrasts with the other cafes in the street and represents the best (and probably the last) of such simple Greek *kafeneion* cul-

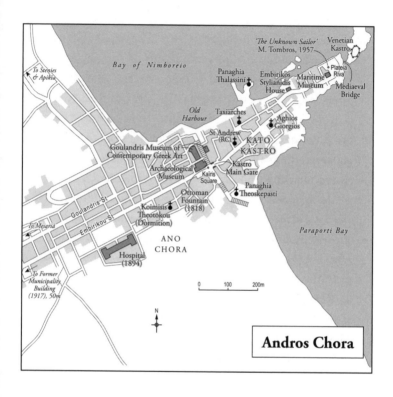

Bay of Nimboreio

To Stenies
& Apikia

'The Unknown Sailor'
M. Tombros, 1957

Venetian
Kastro

Panaghia
Thalassiní

Embirikos
Stylianídis
House

Maritime
Museum

Plateia
Riva

Mediaeval
Bridge

Old
Harbour

Taxiarches

Aghios
Giorgios

St Andrew
(RC)

KATO
KASTRO

Goulandris Museum of
Contemporary Greek Art

Archaeological
Museum

Kaïris
Square

Kastro
Main Gate

Ottoman
Fountain
(1818)

Panaghia
Theoskepastí

To Mesariá

Goulandris St.

Embirikou St.

Koimisis
Theotókou
(Dormition)

ANO
CHORA

Paraporti Bay

Hospital
(1894)

To Former
Municipality
Building
(1917), 50m

0   100   200m

N

Andros Chora

ture. Embirikou Street ends in **Kaïris Square**, named after one of the island's most famous sons, Theophilos Kaïris (1784–1853)—priest, heterodox thinker, polymath, revolutionary and philanthropist. The wide-ranging kind of deism he espoused earned him excommunication and imprisonment twice in his life at the instigation of the authorities of the Orthodox Church. His most concrete project and lasting legacy was to set up a special school for the orphans of the Greek War of Independence, in which his experimental philosophy of education could be practised. Kaïris Square, lined with cafes shaded by planes, centres on an **Ottoman fountain**, which has the reassuring form of a cube with a pyramid on top, surmounted by a Byzantine door-finial and revetted in white and grey marble. It dates from 1818—just three years before the end of the Turkish occupation. The floridly carved marble plaque on its front is typical of late Ottoman '*rococo*' decoration. The fountain has a number of pleasing graffiti carved into the marble on its sides.

In the vicinity are the island's two most important museums: the Archaeological Museum, which gives onto Kaïris Square, and the Goulandris Museum of Contemporary Greek Art lying just below it to the north. The **Archaeological Museum** (*open 8.30–3, closed Mon*) is a small, purpose-built museum with two floors: the upper floor is dedicated to finds from the important early sites of Zagorá (*see pp. 43–45*), Ypsilí and Plaka; the lower floor houses antiquities from the 7th century BC through to the Byzantine period.

Upper floor

Zagorá is one of the most significant sites of the Geometric period to have been excavated in Greece, and the finds exhibited here give a tentative sense of life in the period of the so-called 'Dark Ages', the 9th and 8th centuries BC. The abstract patterns in relief on the large clay *pithoi* are a far cry from the grace and sophistication of much earlier Bronze Age ware, but they have nonetheless a simple and commanding vigour to them which prefigures the power of early Archaic design in Greece. The most beautiful pottery comes from the cemetery and is decorated with patterns of concentric circles—serene, simple and eternal. Some of the exhibits show interesting evidence of the ancient mending of pots with leaden staples. *No. 111* bears a just legible inscription (perhaps of its owner's name) in an early form of the Greek alphabet.

A helpful reconstruction of the temple excavated at Zagorá shows how in this period such a building was really little more than an adapted house, made with finer stonework and with the addition of an altar block.

Ground floor

Most of the ancient finds here are from Palaiopolis (Ancient *Andros*) which was the island's principal centre of habitation from the 7th century BC continuously through to the Arab invasions of the 8th century AD. The first room contains a fine, headless Archaic *kouros* wearing a gently defined *chlamys* (cloak) over a naked torso; this is balanced by the cast of a beautiful *kore* (the original is in Copenhagen) with pleasing, rhythmic folds and pleats in her garment. The lower rooms, however, are dominated by the well-preserved ***Roman copy of the *Hermes* of Praxiteles**. Found in 1833 during the excavations of the *agora* of Palaiopolis, this piece quickly became famous, bringing Ludwig of Bavaria, father of the young King Otho of Greece, all the way to Andros to see it. The ungainly tree-stump support behind the statue's right leg indicates that the piece is a later marble copy of a bronze original, probably of the 4th century BC by Praxiteles. The stylised *contrapposto* and beautiful, but slightly empty, face are similar to other works by Praxiteles (the *Hermes and Dionysos* in Olympia; the Farnese *Hermes* in Rome). What astonishes, however, is the piece's remarkable state of conservation: the head and nose unbroken and integral with the whole; the well-preserved surface which shows the sensitive and fine striations of the sculptor's point, in particular on the back of the shoulders and over the right hip. Faint traces of the original colouring (an element of his works about which Praxiteles was famously demanding) are still visible in the hue of the protected areas around the right thigh, the underside of the belly and possibly in the eyes. The room also contains a finely carved Ionic capital—sensually appealing in its execution, in spite of its abstract form. The high standard of carving is maintained in the vigorous Roman torso of an Artemis figure, with turbulent, wind-tossed robes. Of interest, too, is a Hellenistic grave *stele*, unequivocally 'Christianised' at a later date by the addition of a carved cross with holy monograms.

A stylistic continuity is perceptible as the exhibits pass from the Classical to the early-Christian period; but there is an entirely new sense of pattern and design. Of particular note are the two exquisite marble, 'knotted' **templon columns** (12th century) from the church of Aghios Nikolaos in Mesariá (*see p. 26*).

The *Vassilis and Eliza Goulandris Museum of Contemporary Art (*open June–Sept 10–2, 6–8, except Tues; May & Oct 10–2, Sat, Sun & Mon only*).

The museum is in two buildings: on the left as you descend the stairs is the permanent collection of sculptural works by **Michalis Tombros** (1889–1974) who, though born in Athens, was of Andriot parents from Korthi. The beautiful *Head of a Horse* in the museum's courtyard shows how deeply he was influenced by Classical models, especially the severe style of the pedimental sculptures from Olympia. Tombros studied extensively in Paris and his style consequently became more 'international' in feel. Many of the pieces in the room have a great lyrical beauty, tending on occasions towards abstraction, as for example in his beautiful *Bird and flower flirting* of 1964. There are also paintings by other modern Greek artists exhibited in the spaces here: particularly noteworthy are the whimsical works of **Yannis Gaïtis**, who was also influenced by ancient Greek vase painting, and whose works are an idiosyncratic bridge between modern and ancient.

The building to the right of the steps is on three floors: it houses a changing exhibition space, a useful and well-organised library, and spaces for exhibiting in rotation the works of the permanent collection. There is a clarity and freshness, a pleasing element of whimsy, and an often crystalline sense of design, which mark modern Greek painting out from the frequently underlying aggressiveness of much Northern European modern art. There are always works on show here by **Alekos Fassianós**, who is a fine colourist and a master creator of visual tableaux. His style is unusually detached: his erotic subjects are often strangely un-erotic, and yet unforgettable as images. Also of note are: Panaiotis Tetis's richly colourful frieze-like street scene (1981); a *Deposition* by Yannis Gaïtis (1984); and *The Card Players* (1990) by Pavlos Samios, with a tonality and focus reminiscent of Cézanne.

The distorted perspective of the table in this last painting is taken almost completely for granted nowadays after the overweening naturalism of the 19th century: perhaps the new oddities and deformations of Early Christian art appeared similarly to the eyes of the 5th and 6th centuries, after all the meticulous order of Roman painting. The collection possesses a number of the works of **Yannis Tsarouchis** (1910–89), one of the most thoughtful and restrained of modern Greek artists, who late in his life developed an intensely sensitive observation of the effects of light and shadow on varying surface-textures, worthy of the greatest Spanish masters.

To the south of Kaïris Square, steps lead down to the sandy sweep of Paraporti Bay, passing (to the left) the stately 16th century structure of the church of the Panaghia Theoskepastí. To the east, the main street continues through an arched gateway which was originally the outer entrance to the Venetian walled **Kastro**. Here, in the 19th century, there was a deep declivity, crossed by a draw-bridge, which separated Kato Kastro (through the gate) from Ano Chora (to the west): this can be seen clearly in the beautiful watercolours executed by Arthur Tower on his visit to Andros in 1840. Immediately through the gate, the streets become narrower, although most of the build-ings have been rebuilt in the last century and do not date from the Venetian settlement. In a tiny courtyard off the second street to the left is the **Catholic church of St Andrew**: two eroded faces of saints peer out from the plaster above the main door, and a clearly legible, inscription in Latin proclaims that the church was restored, after its de-struction, to greater glory by Giambattista Crispi in 1749.

Returning to the main artery of Kato Kastro, on the south side is the church of **Aghios Giorgios**. The inte-rior contains many fine *ex votos* of boats; two icons on either side of the central door of the iconostasis, dated to 1820, are worthy of note for the delicacy of their ex-ecution. Many of the houses in the area have arched, upper-storey loggias: the most striking example, which lies beyond the church and the theatre on the left, 75m after the left-hand crook in the street, is the **Embirikos/ Stylianidis mansion**. The street then finishes in an open square, Plateia Riva, at the town's northeastern extremity, dominated by the large, hollow-cast bronze statue of the **Unknown Sailor** (1957) by the Andriot sculptor, Michalis Tombros. The sculpture has been placed awkwardly in such a way that the figure's view of the sea to which he gestures is firmly blocked by the Venetian castle in front. The piece has a heaviness of form and gesture which unavoidably recalls Soviet Realist art. The versatility and skill of this artist is perhaps better appreciated in his more agile works on display at the Goulandris Museum. Looking onto the square is the island's **Maritime Museum** (*open July & Aug 10–1*).

The town ends at this square, but on a rocky outcrop separated by a channel no more than 2m wide, are the remains of the keep and walls of the **Venetian castle or fort**. Built in the early 1200s, this citadel protected from piracy what must have always been a relatively small harbour in the bay of Nimboreio to the north side of Kastro. It was later adapted into the residence of the Sanudo and Dandolo overlords in the 14th century. The core of the main defensive tower still stands to a considerable height;

but the enceinte of walls is mostly gone, and no sign remains of the ancient statue of Hermes over its entrance
mentioned by a visitor in the 18th century. The most
conspicuous and beautiful remnant today is the steeply
arched bridge which connects the islet to the promontory. The steepness of its supporting arch derives from
the projection of rock from which it springs on the far
side and which determines the high curve of the center-
ing required for its construction.

Leaving Chora to the west, just before the junction of
the road to Korthi and Ormos Korthiou, is the **cemetery**
of the town. This is one of the finest in the Cyclades, with
beautiful cenotaphs to the Goulandris and Embirikos dy-
nasties, and a memorable monument to Yannis Moraïtis,
who died in London in 1925.

CENTRAL ANDROS

THE MESARIA VALLEY, STENIES & THE BISTI-MOUVELA TOWER

The Mesariá Valley is a landscape of unspoiled villages, springs and fertile gardens: it also contains a number of interesting and ancient churches. The villages are close and distances are small: this is an area which is peaceful and pleasant for walking.

Entering the village of Mesariá from Chora, the large church of **Aghios Nikolaos** is on your right; it was from the former church on this site that the magnificent knotted columns in the Archaeological Museum were taken. The existing church was radically restored in the 19th century but it possesses some particularly **fine marble decoration** around and above the three exterior west doors—work executed in 1734 in the workshops of Chios: the south doorway, on the other hand, is surrounded by a 12th century marble door-frame from the original foundation. Other interesting marble work is seen across the road at the tiny church of the **Taxiarchis Michaïl**, which lies in a peaceful setting a short way down the path opposite the south side of Aghios Nikolaos. Here the west door has a rare and intricate marble surround of the 12th century with carved animals and foliage. The original 12th century church was a domed Greek-cross shape; the narthex was added much later, at which time the west door-frame was moved to the new entrance. The quality of the masonry here is also remarkable. Notice the fine abstract orientalising pattern of a sunburst on the exterior of the north facet of the apse, and the unusual regimented dressing and dimpling of the grey stone in the north wall and narthex. The north door has clearly been filled in: in front of it (on the outside) is evidence of a baptismal pool or a porched well which may well even predate the 12th century building.

West of Mesariá is the village of **Ménites**. Springs seem to be rising everywhere here, although they are fewer now than before: huge plane trees profit from their waters. At the centre of the village is a row of six lion's heads spouting water: such fountains are distantly reminiscent of their Hellenistic forebears, such as the one at Ialysos on Rhodes. Above them and right below the church are yet more springs emerging this time from early 19th century Byzantine-style marble-fronts. The whole hillside bears water: at **Strapouriés** (to the east) there are a number of water mills. More springs rise under the 13th century church of the Panaghia in **Mesáthouri**, which has a number of original marble embellishments built into it. At **Ypsiloú** is another 13th century church (of the Taxi-arches) with similar Greek-cross plan and a cupola on two columns and two piers. Both of these two churches have been enlarged and altered in the last century. The earliest and best preserved of these churches of the mid-dle-Byzantine era however, is at the western extremity of the valley at **Melída**. The church, once again dedicated to the **Taxiarchis Michaïl**, is visible and signposted from the main road, 3km northeast of the Stavropeda junction on the west coast. It dates from the 11th century, and its octagonal cupola drum and the faceted apses have beauti-ful *cloisonné* masonry, which contrasts with the rougher masonry of the body of the church. The northeast corner contains an ancient marble block, which has been im-mured upside down; it bears an antique inscription which appears to be an artist's signature of a work of which this block was possibly the pedestal.

Returning to Chora, the road north from the town leads to Steniés and Apíkia, past the unspoiled pebble beach of Giália. **Steniés** provides a good cross-section of Andriot architecture: it is a village of great beauty. There are many stately, neoclassical mansions with gardens of cypress, lemon and fruit-trees. The streets are without traffic; the sound is only of running water, gushing from a spring by a central washing area, shaded by a building above. The luminous interior of the Metropolitan Church of St George contains some unusual, academic murals by Kostantinos Mavropoulos of the 1930s. Two hundred and fifty metres west of the village is the **Bisti-Mouvela Tower**: its stands in a state of abandon with collapsed ceilings and broken floors. This grim and imposing, fortified house of the mid 17th century gives a clear idea of the real fear of piracy which prevailed at that time: the walls are of impregnable thickness, there are few windows (and only slits for ventilation on the lower levels), and the machicolation above the entrance door allowed for boiling liquids to greet the unwelcome visitor.

FROM APIKIA TO YPSILI

From Stenies, the road rises towards Apíkia passing another large, abandoned stone mansion: as it crosses the stream on the last bend before the village, steps to the left lead up to the chapel of Aghios Nikolaos which is part church, part cave, carved out of the cliff—very probably the 'christianising' of a pagan shrine to Pan. The **Sáriza spring** rises in Apikia; its water gushes from a marble lion's mouth just above the *Pigi Sariza Hotel* in the village. The water is famous, and is bottled and marketed in many parts of

Greece and is believed to have notable therapeutic qualities. Andros has a lot of water and most of it is good; but
the Sariza water is remarkably well-rounded, and noticea-
bly sweeter than most. It has a delicate mineral flavour and
is worth any journey made here to taste it. From Apikia,
just before the spring, a foot-path leads west up the scenic
and unspoiled *Pithara Valley. It is a strange and pleasing
sensation to be on an island in the middle of the sea and
yet to be able to walk beside a mountain stream with waterfalls and shaded pools. This is a delightful ramble, and
rich in interest for its bird and butterfly life.

A kilometre and a half above Apikia, the road passes
the abandoned monastery of **Aghia Irini**, high up on the
hillside. Suggestively nestled inside the massive, ruined
stone walls of the monastery, the church, which is still
in occasional use, dates from the 18th century; its inside
is plain with a carved white marble templon screen. The
monastery's spring still flows, and feeds fig and other fruit
trees, which grow amongst the ruins of the finely constructed and vaulted buildings of the former monastic
quarters. A different scene is presented by the **monastery
of Aghios Nikolaos**, which the road passes after a further
2km (*1.5km down signed track to right*). This is very much
a living and working monastery of almost unseemly prosperity, with meticulously pointed stone-work, polished

brass and new plants. The *catholicon*, whose foundation is of 1560 though completely restored in 1757–60, is in a curious striated masonry of grey-white marble from the north of the island and a yellow, Skyros sandstone. Only the narthex contains substantial remains of its wall-paintings, but the undressed stonework of the interior shows the fine skeleton of the construction. The interior bears witness to the monastery's continuing vitality in the numerous *ex votos* hanging from the silver candelabra—ships and sailing boats dedicated by mariners, a TIR lorry, 3 fine ostrich eggs …

From here the road climbs and then descends into an unexpected area of fertility and scattered villages, Arnes, Katakilos, Revmata—all verdant, well-watered and mostly unvisited. After 24km the road reaches the west coast at Batsí, a pleasant town built up around a small cove and harbour, with shops, tavernas, cafés and hotels. Batsi is Andros's principal tourist centre. Three kilometres south of Batsi, the coast road passes the plateau of **Ypsilí** on the seaward side. The archaeological site here (*currently closed for excavation and restoration*) has revealed another Geometric period settlement of the 9th and 8th centuries BC, comparable and contemporary with that at Zagorá (*see p. 43*). The wall of the acropolis is clearly visible and has been cleared from the front side on the east, facing the road. To the south are the foundations of a number of dwellings. In the centre of the plateau circumscribed by the wall are the stone foundations of an early 6th century BC **temple** on the plan of a *megaron*: the stone 'furniture' uncovered by archaeologists in the sanctum (wall-benches and tables) has given rise to the suggestion—unusual, given the position and site—that this was a place of chthonic cult, possibly of Demeter. Perhaps the best idea of the layout of the whole site can be obtained by going a little way up the road to Alikandro and Aprovato (*junction opposite site*) and viewing the area from above.

PALAIOPOLIS

After a further 5km towards the south, the coast road comes to *****Palaiopolis**—site of the city of Ancient *Andros* and political centre of the island for 1,300 years from the 7th century BC through to the 8th century AD. As so often with ancient Greek foundations the siting of the city is splendid and beautiful, and it is this which provides more interest for the visitor than the somewhat meagre archaeological remains. The meticulously explained displays in the new museum beside the road which present the site and its finds very succinctly compensate for the scarcity of remains.

The ancient city was laid out on the steep slopes of a theatre-shaped declivity in the western face of the island's highest mountains (Mts Petalos and Kouvara), which reach their summits almost directly above the town. Two main gorges with waterfalls cut through the slopes: in the spring the southern torrent pours dramatically in a slender fall straight over the ridge above the town. These streams have been responsible for the silting up of the ancient harbour below and the burying of much of the city's (lower) public areas under alluvial soil. The position is very protected; it faces west and looks towards the Attic mainland and the other northwestern islands of the Cyclades.

Exploration of the site is not easy, and it can only be reached on foot. Two paths with steps descend to the harbour and beach: one down the southeastern perimeter, the other down the northwestern side. On either descent, clearly visible from above when the water is calm, is the submerged harbour mole which projects into the sea at an oblique angle and whose 'elbow' appears above water about 20m out from the shore. At shore level, the ruined building standing at the point where the south east steps end has a finely inscribed ancient stone built into its structure; behind the north end of the bay where the mole meets the shore are the overgrown **remains of Roman baths**; and on the rocky outcrop which divides the bay to the south, there appears to have been a watch-tower, suggested by the large fashioned blocks of green and white marble on top of the rocks. It is not easy to penetrate the interior of the site, but a small area of excavation in the centre of the first 'tier' of the hill has revealed marble paving and the base of a stoa-like build-ing of the city's *agora*, which occupied this area behind the harbour. Re-ascending by the northwestern path, you pass on the left (approximately two thirds of the way up) the re-mains of an **Early Christian basilica**, with a number of fine monolithic columns of Karystos marble lying nearby. Most impressive of all—but hardest to locate and to reach—are the massive late Classical **retaining walls** which reinforced the terracing of the city where the slope is at its steepest. These are made of huge, dressed, marble blocks, which, on occasions, exceed 2m in length. They are located (down to the right, below where the northwest path levels out) amongst dense olive and cypress groves on the northern edge of the northern gorge, about 80–100m below the level of the modern road.

The piecemeal and intermittent character of excavations which have taken place here, and the speed with which na-ture has reclaimed areas explored in the past, mean that, of the theatre, the *gymnasium*, and the temple (probably of Apollo) in the mid-eastern section of the valley, and of the acropolis above and to the west, virtually nothing is visible on site. For this reason a visit to the excellent museum is very helpful.

The **Palaiopolis Museum** (*open 10–3, closed Mon*) is a choice collection of remarkable pieces found on the site, as well as some clear explanatory material. Of the tiny, ancient personalia which the museum exhibits, particularly interesting and rare are: the small, articulated puppet (*no. 43*); a Hellenistic ring with a fine *intaglio* of a Nike in cornelian (*no. 105a*), and a 6th century BC solid bronze figure of a dressed *kouros*. (Solid bronze figures such as this are difficult to cast well because of the danger of deformation which can occur on cooling as the material contracts unevenly according to its thickness. This potential distortion is reduced to a minimum in hollow-casting because of the uniform thickness of the metal. Hollow-casting (by the 'lost wax' method) was also desirable to minimise the quantity and cost of primary materials required, but it could only be effected on much larger pieces. Figurines in bronze of this small size are nearly always cast solid.) Also of the Archaic period (6th century BC) is a beautiful fragment of **Bellerophon and Pegasus* (*no. 163*); and of comparable sensitivity of stone-carving, but of a later style and date, is the fragment from a marble **figurine of Artemis** (*no.174*). The large **lion** (*no. 168*), in which earlier stylisation has given way to a new and unerring naturalism, is a Classical piece of the late 5th century BC which probably was created to be a grave-marker. *Nos 175 & 176* are also fragments of grave stones: they possess the common iconography of the three-legged table and the coiled serpent. The museum also has some particularly interesting inscriptions: these sometimes provide valuable historical information (*see no. 187/8*, which appears to refer to a benefaction to the city made by Eumenes, king of Pergamon); on other occasions they can provide good insight into Greek cults as is the case with *no. 209*, which is a partially legible **poem spoken by the goddess Isis**. In it, the goddess herself—a divinity from Egypt who in her compassion and suffering is a precursor of so many female saints and even of aspects of the Virgin Mary—speaks in the first person about herself and her gifts to humanity.

THE SOUTH OF THE ISLAND

MONI PANACHRANTOU &
APANO KASTRO

The mountain slopes on the southern side of the Mesariá Valley are crowned by the whitewashed bulk of *Moni Panachrantou (*closed 1–4.30: 2 hrs pleasant walk from Chora; also reachable by car*). The climb up to the monastery affords inspiring views of the valley, Chora and the sea, and passes several abandoned towers and hermitages clinging to the side of the mountain. One of these, about two thirds of the way up, is easily accessible and shows clearly the characteristic layout of such buildings: animal byres at the lowest levels with stone mangers; the family habitation on the main floor above, with fireplace and huge, stone-slab floors; and finally drying-lofts and dovecot in the roof above—all executed in finely packed, small-stone masonry.

The monastery itself, built like a fortress with an animated roof-line and spectacular views, owes its site to the numerous springs that rise here. Tradition gives its foundation to the austere and inflexible, soldier-Emperor of Byzantium, Nikephoros II Phokas, in the second half of the 10th century; but almost everything visible today is from the 17th century, except for the *catholicon*, dedicated to the Dormition of the Virgin, which is probably 200 years earlier, even though its entrance door has a fine 17th century marble frame. The monastery is entered through a succession of courtyards and arched passages, full of trees, palms, plants and the sound of running water everywhere. Once home to over 200 monks, there is now only one permanent monastic resident. The interior of the *catholicon* contains some fine wall-paintings which are now unfortunately very damaged and hard to read. But the interior's quite unexpected beauty lies in the magnificent *templon* screen which is revetted (in its lower areas) with a splendid array of Ottoman, Iznik tiles of the late 16th century. This is high Iznik-work of great beauty, dating from the period of the first experimentation in three or more colours. These tiles were a not insignificant gift made to the monastery from Constantinople, perhaps by the Ecumenical Patriarch Dionysos III. They alone make a visit here worth the effort.

Just below the monastery is an 18th century chapel (1759) by a dried-up spring, with a large and curiously-fashioned washing area in front.

Above the monastery the road crosses a watershed and

the landscape changes considerably. A high plateau opens to the south with spectacular views to Tinos; three impressive limestone caps, or 'tors', march in line across a rugged landscape, checkered with miles and miles of the characteristic Andriot walling.

THE FIELD-WALLS OF ANDROS

The hillsides of Andros, especially in the south of the island, are covered everywhere by the island's own peculiar and very original kind of dry-stone walling. These walls, which separate areas of pasture and run for miles across the landscape, are characterised by the inclusion of large, flat, roughly triangular-shaped pieces of schist fixed vertically into the ground every 2m or so parallel to the line of the wall, while the rest of the wall is composed of small, narrow stone in-fill between these orthostats. This represented a way of economising on stone-breaking while giving a more robust structure to the walls. But it also gave rise to an effect of great beauty, in particular when the light is low and the vertical slabs reflect the sun giving the impression that the contours of the landscape are draped with loose-linked necklaces. At other moments, in a different light, they can seem less welcoming—more like rows of teeth. This method of construction is also found in places on Tinos and on other Cycladic islands, but nowhere is it as plentiful and meticulously executed as on Andros.

Below and to the south is the Dipotamos Valley, scattered with villages and with **water-mills**. One of these mills, somewhat restored, lies just upstream of the junction of the road from Panachrantos with the Chora/Korthi road, near Exo Vouni. There is a shallow, lined, retaining-pool (about 40m long) above the mill, with a plug which can be drawn mechanically, by means of a pivot handle, from below. This allows the water to descend a narrow tower into the chamber underneath where there is a horizontally mounted turbine which turns the mill. There are many other mills in the valley.

At Kochilou, 1.7km from the Exo Vouni junction, a small road is signposted to the left to the 'Panaghia'. This leads up towards the summit of the easternmost of the limestone 'tors'. After the road ends, steps continue up to the recently rebuilt church of the Panaghia. Beyond it are the remains of the Venetian castle and fortifications of **Apano Kastro**. Some time between the abandoning of the ancient Greek city of Andros at Palaiopolis on the west coast in the 8th century AD, and the beginning of settlement on the promontory of the modern-day Chora in the 13th century, this spectacular site emerged as the island's safest refuge in times of danger, although the castle we see the remains of today was built only at the end of that long period. There are clear remains of cisterns to the left of the path and remnants of the fortification wall. A bastion crowned the farthest end of the ridge: as you climb up, with the wall on your right, the marks of the door fixtures can be seen in the stone 'steps'. This was the island's final and impregnable refuge: it could probably communicate by signals with the fortress of Xoburgo on Tinos which is visible from here, and could house a large population during a siege for as long as its cisterns could provide sufficient water. The *views of the island and of the others scattered in the sea around are unforgettable.

AROUND KORTHI

From Kochilou the road descends to Ormos Korthiou through a chain of villages—Stavrós, Episkopeío, Lardiá, Rogó (often referred to collectively as '**Palaiokastro**')— all of which have many abandoned old houses typical of the island's vernacular architecture. The village of

Kórthi, 2km behind the wide sweep of its bay, likewise
has a number of stone towers and mansions of the 17th
and 18th centuries—strongly built for defensive reasons,
but perforated with windows that render them more light
and habitable: perhaps the finest example stands amid
cypresses and olives in the valley just below **Aidónia**, the
village which clings to the easternmost end of the slope of
the mountain to the south of the bay. Its principal church
is dedicated to the **Forty Martyrs of Sebaste** (just to the
west of the main modern church). It has a pure interior
with a fine stone *templon* screen and adapted ancient columns in the nave. It took its present form in the early
18th century, although it incorporates elements from an
earlier building. Over the outside of the west door (above
and to the right) is an unusual and notable **marble icon**,
carved in folkloric style in the early 1730s: below the
Almighty in a nimbus, are the forty semi-naked saints,
disposed in rows, all with their arms crossed in front
of them. (The same theme—of the Forty Martyrs—is
repeated in the icons inside the church.) In addition to
the frequent marble screens on the island, such marble
plaques are a particular feature of the art of 18th century Andros, where churches also often bear elaborately
carved founder's slabs above their entrances. A little
further north in **Ano Kórthi**, to the east of the village's

plateia and fountain, is the church of **Aghios Nikolaos**, next to a fine, ruined Venetian mansion. This is a 12th century church in origin: its pure form, with a dome supported on two columns and two piers, is a prototype for many later churches on the island.

ZAGORA & STROPHILAS

After Aipatia, which has a number of beautiful dovecotes (*see box pp. 85–88*), the road climbs out of the valley towards the west coast and after 13km joins the island's principal road at the junction of Stavropeda. Five hundred metres to the south of this junction is the isolated church of Aghia Triada: from here a path leads down to the **archaeological site of Zagorá**. (*Access to the site is difficult, and takes 50 mins each way: a stick is necessary to clear cobwebs and vegetation along the pathway. The path goes up the side of the church and branches to the right: after 15mins, at a T-junction, descend steeply to the right and then follow round to the left. The path skirts the slope of the mountain: it is best not to leave this path until you see a clear perpendicular track leading straight down to the neck of the headland.*)

The site was first excavated in the 1960s by the University of Sydney and the artefacts found here are now in the archaeological museum in Andros (*see above*). Zagorá's heyday was in the Late Geometric period, between 850 and 700 BC, though there is evidence of habitation as far back as the 10th century BC. There are not that many significant sites from this period in Greece; hence the importance of the excavations here.

From the path the layout of the site soon becomes clear: the neck of the headland, cut transversely by the remarkable man-made fortifications of the 9th century BC, and then the promotory itself, with its surrounding escarpment forming a natural curtain of fortification on the seaward sides. The foundations of houses and buildings within this perimeter can also be seen. The choice of site is clear, too, with its commanding views of Gyaros, Syros and Kea, a tiny port far below, and considerable natural protection; no source of water, however, is evident today. The site itself is a little confusing, not least because there is also some more recent walling and building which can cause confusion with the ancient remains.

The **fortification wall** is best preserved at the southern end. Constructed meticulously of schist rock, it was probably about 2.5m high, and varies in thickness from 2–4m. A **gate** is visible with the base of a **bastion** to its north: this took care of the exposed right-hand side of an external attacker. The town appears to have grown organically with no clear predetermined plan. The remains of the houses are mainly concentrated in the centre of the site, though a number of buildings interestingly abut the inside of the walls and may have been used partly as magazines for defensive material. The houses would have been constructed of schist, with baked mud roofs over wooden beams. In the centre, at almost the highest point, the foundations of a **temple** are recognisable: there is a *pronaos*, and a *naos* with the base for what was possibly a cult statue visible in the middle. This design indicates that we are looking here at a much later temple of the Archaic or Classical era, which was probably built over the site of an earlier place of worship of the Geometric era, and which was maintained after the general abandonment of the settlement. It is oriented on a due north/south axis. Nearby is a complex of houses and rooms—one with a central hearth and benches around it, all still clearly visible.

Important evidence of **early prehistoric settlements** has also been found slightly further south on the headland above the bay of Plaka, and just to the north of Zagorá on the promontory of **Stróphilas**, where one of the largest Neolithic settlements (5th millennium BC) in the Aegean has been brought to light. The settlement was protected by substantial walls; excavation has revealed the bases of large buildings, and of a very early sanctuary comprising

a large hall (c. 100 sq.m), with a circular stone construction at its centre. Perhaps the most significant find from
the site has been the variety of shallow-carved rock-art
of the late 5th and early 4th millennia BC, which is found
on many of the blocks and flagstones and depicts ships,
animals and various abstract designs. This, together with
the quality of the artefacts found, gives a very clear sense
of both the sophistication of the culture to be found here
so early, as well as of the importance of this stretch of the
coast of Andros in the Aegean world of the Chalcolithic
period (4500–3200 BC). Access to these sites is either officially restricted (Stróphilas) or difficult (Plaka), and they
are of generally greater academic significance than visual
interest.

THE NORTH OF THE ISLAND

ZOODOCHOS PIGI MONASTERY &
THE TOWER OF AGHIOS PETROS

On an eminence almost due north of Batsi and inland of
the coast is the **monastery of the Zoödochos Pigi**. (*2km
north of Batsi on the main coast road a sign points inland
to 'Tis Aghias', which is reached after a climb of 3.4km. The
monastery, closed 1–4.30, is also referred to as 'Aghias Monastery'.*) Vast and fortress-like, this is a bleak building in
a bleak setting. An air of tristesse prevails and only two
melancholy nuns now inhabit what was once a teeming
monastery. There is no vegetation, just wonderful, open
views to the sea on both sides of the island. The monastery
buildings, which mostly date from the 18th and 19th centuries (although the foundation appears from documents
to pre-date 1400), are a vivid contrast to the Panachrantos and Aghios Nikolaos monasteries: here there is no in-
timacy or joyous greenery in the spaces—just one small
spring. A few fragments of ancient marble and a couple
of column bases have been assembled in the courtyard,
but it is not clear from where. Inside the *catholicon*, the
templon screen is the most interesting element: the lower

part is beautiful, and made from a warm, reddish stone, possibly *portasanta* marble from Chios; above it is a heavy wooden iconostasis. The few wall-paintings remaining are too damaged to date with any certainty. Their surface has been regularly chipped and dimpled with a sharp tool: this was done when a new layer of plaster for fresco painting was to be superimposed on the existing one: the chipped depressions helped the new plaster to 'key into' the surface of the old.

A further 3.5km north, on the very southern edge of Gavrio, a road inland followed immediately again by a turning to the south, leads to one of the island's most important antiquities, the *tower of Aghios Petros. (The tower is visible from a bend in the road, and a track leads 200m across the hillside to it. Access is not particularly easy, however.)* This is one of the best preserved cylindrical ancient Greek towers in the Aegean, comparable with the towers at Heimaros on Naxos and at Darkanon on Ikaria. Together they constitute the three finest examples of something which quickly becomes a familiar element of the ancient landscape for the observant traveller around the islands.

HELLENISTIC TOWERS

The free-standing and isolated stone tower—of which the Aghios Petros tower on Andros is an exceptionally good example—is a phenomenon of ancient architecture that is encountered all over the Aegean Islands, especially in the Cyclades. Beautiful in themselves for the calm meticulousness and strength of their construction, the towers constituted a versatile kind of structure, easily adaptable both to civic and military purposes. Most appear to have been erected between the 4th and 2nd centuries BC. They were generally constructed in large, rectangular blocks of dressed ashlar masonry, which in the case of the cylindrical towers were cut with precision on the curve of the overall circumference. Most possessed internal staircases and wooden floors, and some had relatively large window apertures. Given their height (which often may have reached 20m or more) these towers have tended to fall victim to earthquakes: with this in mind, their builders gave them very sound foundations which, in some cases, are all that remain of them.

The towers are so numerous, and their sites and

positions so varied, that there is no single purpose
or shape which was common to them all. Many—
such as that at Drakanon on Ikaria—were undoubt-
edly built for defensive reasons, and, with prominent
and visible sites, may have been part of a signalling
network which could quickly disseminate warning
of an imminent danger over large distances and to
many communities. But the density of towers on islands such as Siphnos, Seriphos and Thasos, which
had important mining installations, suggests that
many of them were constructed to guard the mines
and the ore they produced. A final group—including
the two rectangular towers at Aghia Marina on Kea
and at Aghia Triada on Amorgos—are sited lower
down in valleys, and must have watched over areas
of rich agricultural production. Even so, the exact
way in which these buildings functioned (for storage, for garrisons, for refuge, for look out, etc.) is
still not clear in every case; nor is it obvious what
the nature of the danger was to these commercial interests which would require such an expensive and
laborious construction for their protection, or could
in the end best be deterred by this particular kind of

fortress tower. Ancient texts are silent on the subject. Few of the towers (Aghia Marina on Kea is a notable exception) appear to have been used or adapted to different uses in later centuries. Most now stand today to a height that rarely exceeds 3 or 4m.

At Aghios Petros the tower still stands to over 21m, and has a slightly tapering diameter of between 9 and 9.5m. It is constructed of large, individually fashioned, blocks of a warm, pinkish limestone and has remarkably survived the centuries of earth-tremors which are a constant feature of the Aegean area. A massive spiral staircase, still partly in evidence, communicated between its four (or five) upper storeys, each of which had a large framed window looking south towards the sea. A vertical stone blind projects on the east side of one of the upper windows. Supports for the first wooden floor can be seen 3–3.5m above the top of the lower chamber. The interior is dressed in places with smaller, regular stones. The building can probably be dated to the 4th century BC.

Two features of this tower stand out. First, the impressive and **finely corbelled dome** at the base of the tower, which has all the appearance of a Mycenaean burial chamber, but which is constructed in a kind of masonry which is clearly of much later date. There is a perceptible change in stonework, most visible on the outside, between this lower area and the cylindrical tower above: the lunettes which pierce the chamber also appear possibly to have been cut later. The second peculiar feature lies in the three straight, vertical, shallow-cut, recessed bands which run the whole height of the outside of the tower from top to ground level. What these were for is not clear: possibly they were necessary for fixing the scaffolding during construction; less probably for holding a clay down-pipe, as has been suggested.

The surrounding area was not only vital to the agriculture of the island in ancient times, but ancient iron mines have also been located in the valley. The Aghios Petros tower probably played a part in the overseeing and protecting of these activities, and watching over the manual workforce which would have consisted mainly of slaves, prisoners and conscripts. The tower, though high, is not logically positioned for communications and look-out and it does not appear to have clear sight-lines to other towers in the area that we know of.

After Aghios Petros the road continues east across the island, through tranquil landscape to Vitali village (after 6km) and the perfect and unvisited, sandy beach of Piso Vitali below (after 8km). Below the road are visible the atmospheric ruins of the **monastery of the Pantocrator,** also known as the monastery of Sotiras. This is an area where *Hypericum delphicum*, or St John's-wort, can be found. In cracks on the upper screes, the rare, very pale bluey-white flowered *Campanula sartorii*, which is endemic to Tinos and Andros, can also be seen. It is often thought to be a survivor from pre-glacial times.

THE NORTH OF THE ISLAND

Gávrio is Andros's only active port: the regular ferries for Rafina, and for Tinos and Mykonos, all stop here. North of Gávrio, the geography of the island has a very different feel—wide-open, windswept uplands, with fewer and more sparsely inhabited villages: its farthest valleys and moors have something of the feel of the north of Scotland about them. The road up the west coast passes numerous beaches and coves, and has fine views towards Attica and Euboea. At its northern end is **Makrotantalo Castle**, a small ruined Venetian tower which marked the western entrance to the 'Doro Passage', or Kaphireas Straits, between Euboea and Andros.

On the main road north, shortly after Epano Fellos, a settlement which has open views and a good spring, is a track to the right for Amólochos. Here, immediately on the right, are two quarries of local marble: the veined, grey-white stone is in places similar to the *cipollino* marbles of the Karystos area on Euboea, but it lacks their richness of colour and fineness of veining. Beyond the quarries, the road climbs to **Amólochos**. Some of the abandoned stone houses here bear witness to the former prosperity of this settlement, which lived 200 years ago on silk production. Today there remain only the magnificent, open views towards one of wildest corners of the Aegean Sea.

PRACTICAL INFORMATION

845 01/2 **Andros**: area 383 sq.km; perimeter 176km; resident population 9,285; max. altitude 997m. **Port Authorities**: T. 22820 22250. **Travel and information**: Porto Andros Travel, T. 22820 71222, fax. 71542, www.andros.gr

ACCESS

Access to the island, which has no airport, is from the Attic port of Rafina by two twice daily services—regular car-ferry (2 hr) and high-speed ferry (1 hr). Boats dock at the port of Gavrio on the north west coast of the island, 33km. from the island's capital, Andros Chora.

LODGING

There are small hotels of reasonable quality in Gávrio, Batsi, Chora and at Ormos Korthi. At Apikia, beside the Sariza springs, is the fairly basic **Hotel Pigi Sariza**, which offers tranquillity and the springs' excellent waters (*T. 22820 23799, fax 23899*). In the centre of Chora is the **Archontiko Eleni Hotel** in a restored, neoclassical mansion once belonging to the Embirikos family. It is near the top of the town's main street, and is open all through the year (*T. 22820 23471 & 22270, fax 22294*).

EATING

Although the surroundings seem unpromising, the tiny **Madoula Restaurant** on the front at Nimboreio serves fresh, well-prepared dishes. A reasonable variety of good, principally fish and vegetable dishes can also be found at **Ononas**, a small *mezedopoleion* right down in the corner of the harbour below the north side of Kato Kastro in Chora. On Giália beach, below Steniés, is the **Taverna Gialia** offering good food in a pleasant setting. Two rural restaurants deserve special mention for their excellent local fare: the panoramic *Taverna Bozaki in Ypsiloú, and **Taverna Kossis** on a wild hillside, north of Epáno Fellos in the north of the island. Andros is famous for its spicy sausages, and an omelette-like dish combining them with egg and potato, called *frutália*. Its almond biscuits called *amigdalotá* are a delight with which to round off a meal.

FURTHER READING

Aegean Days, by J. Irving Manatt (originally published by John Murray, London 1913) is an interesting 'period' piece with a sensitive evocation (in Part I) of Andros at the turn of the last century.

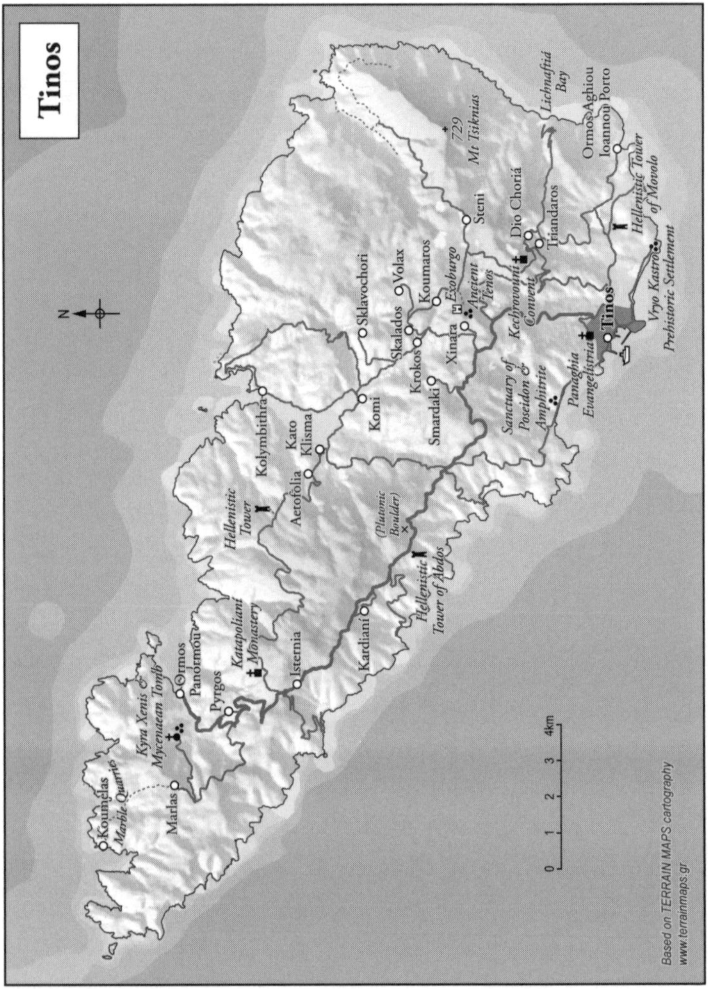
Tinos
N
Koumelas
Marble Quarries
Marlas
Kyra Xenis & Mycenaean Tomb
Pyrgos
Ormos Panormou
Katapoliani Monastery
Isternia
Kardiani
Hellenistic Tower of Abdos
Hellenistic Tower
Aetofolia
Kato Klisma
Kolymbithra
(Platonic Boulder)
Komi
Sklavochori
Smardaki
Krokos
Skalados
Volax
Koumaros
Xinara
Exoburgo
Ancient Tenos
Steni
729 Mt Tsiknias
Sanctuary of Poseidon & Amphitrite
Kechrovouni Convent
Dio Choriá
Triandaros
Panaghia Evangelistria
Tinos
Vryo Kastro Prehistoric Settlement
Hellenistic Tower of Movolo
Ormos Aghiou Ioannou Porto
Lichnaftiá Bay
0 1 2 3 4km
Based on TERRAIN MAPS cartography
www.terrainmaps.gr

TINOS

There is a restless energy to Tinos—not just in the ebb and flow of pilgrims who come at all times of the day and the year to pay their respects at the church of the Evangelistria to one of Greece's holiest icons, but in the more general sense of a creative activity both past and present on the island. Wherever one looks, the terracing of the hillsides reflects the work of centuries of dedicated human cultivation. Beautiful dovecotes dot every corner of the island's landscape, their intricate design arising from a spirit of architectural playfulness which goes well beyond the demands of mere necessity. There are lovingly carved marble details on the houses—fanlights, plaques, balconies and, in the case of the 'marble village' of Pyrgos, almost every element of municipal furniture. And there is a calmly bustling activity to the island's intimate rural villages which contrasts with those on many of the other islands where a rudderless lassitude brought by tourism can sometimes prevail. Even the sky above Tinos seems constantly riven with the darting flight of white doves; the winds, propelled by Aeolus whose palace was believed by the Ancients to be on Mount Tsiknias in the southeast of the island, are

rarely still; and the land itself—especially in the valley
at Volax—bears the scars of unusual geological turbu-
lence.

Tinos is often mistakenly overlooked because it is on
the route for more popular Cycladic Islands and because
its port lacks some of the charm that others possess; but
it is nonetheless an island remarkably rich in a wide variety of interest and history. It combines being the most
important destination for local Greek religious tourism
and pilgrimage in the country, with the pleasure afforded
by a 'living', unselfconscious island, largely untouched
by foreign tourism. The Orthodox religious tradition on
Tinos is strong and is centred on the ornate Evangelistria
church, with its high quality of Byzantine chant; but the
island is also home to the Aegean's largest Catholic population. In consequence an Italianate style permeates the
island's architecture. There is also a strong tradition of local folk-art, especially in stone-sculpting which is fuelled
by the island's deposits of fine marble, and has seen considerable importance in the last two centuries. The island
is the birth-place of three of Greece's greatest academic
painters and sculptors of the 19th century—Gyzis, Lytras
and Chalepas.

The stone-working tradition on Tinos is a living con-
nection with ancient practices. In fact the feeling of con-

tinuity between past and present on the island is remarkably strong. In Antiquity, the waters off Tinos were home to one of the most important cults of the divinities of the sea, centred on the Hellenistic sanctuary of Poseidon and Amphitrite, just north of Chora, where the yearly Poseidonia festivals were celebrated. Strabo says that multitudes would take part in these celebrations. It is just the same today during the major feasts of the Virgin when the pilgrimage church of the Evangelistria is thronged with celebrants from all over Greece.

HISTORY & LEGEND

The island was anciently called *Ophiousa* ('abounding in snakes'); and the name *Tenos* may derive from the Phoenician word '*tanoth*' or '*tenok*', meaning a serpent. A celebrated temple was dedicated to Poseidon who was credited with sending storks to eradicate the snakes.

The conical hill of Vryokastro to the south of the port of Tinos was an important centre in prehistoric times and flourished in the Middle Bronze Age; and a small *tholos* tomb in the north of the island is evidence of a later, Mycenaean presence on the island. Around 950 BC the island was settled by Ionians from Caria. The main settlement on Tinos in the 7th and 6th centuries BC then became the slopes of the granite outcrop of Xoburgo in the centre of the island, above which the Venetians were much later to build their principal fortress. In 480 BC the Tenians were forced to serve in the Persian fleet of Xerxes against Greece, but their trireme defected to the Greeks before the Battle of Salamis, providing crucial information about Persian intentions (Herodotus, VIII, 82 ff.). For this service the island's name was inscribed, along with the names of the others who participated in the Greek victory, on the bronze Serpentine Column of Delphi which is now in the Hippodrome in Istanbul. In the 4th century BC, the city was relocated from Xoburgo to the site of the present town of Tinos. At the same time the sanctuary of Poseidon and Amphitrite was founded nearby.

In the wake of the capture of Constantinople in the Fourth Crusade in 1204, Tinos was assigned to the Latin Emperor by the Deed of Partition. The island was claimed by Marco Sanudo, nephew of the aged Doge Dandolo who had led the Crusade, and was subsequently given by him to Andrea and Geremia Ghisi to rule as vassals. In 1390 Tinos, together with Mykonos, was bequeathed to the state of Venice. In 1407 the fiefdom of Tinos was awarded by Venice to Giovanni Querini, lord of the island of Astypalaia (Stampalia), but after his fall from favour the island was subsequently ruled by a Rector appointed regularly by the Council of the Serene Republic. The island remained a Venetian territory right down to 1715, and was the longest held of all Venice's possessions in the Aegean. As a consequence it has the largest Roman Catholic population of all the Cyclades and still has its own Roman Catholic bishop, convents, schools and churches. After no fewer than eleven unsuccessful attempts, the Turks eventually captured the island in 1715, granting a number of privileges to the island under their rule. The raising of the flag of independence at Pyrgos in March 1821, however, provoked Turkish reprisals. In this highly charged atmosphere, a miraculous icon of the Virgin was unearthed in 1823 on Tinos, at a site revealed by a nun who had had a vision of the Virgin Mary. The cult of the icon has since made Tinos a place of national pilgrimage, not only at the major feasts of the Annunciation (25 March) and the Assumption (15 August), but throughout the year. On the day of the Feast of the Assumption in 1940, a Greek cruiser, the *Helle*, was torpedoed by an Italian submarine in the port of Tinos on the eve of the outbreak of war between Greece and Italy. During the German occupation, there was heavy loss of life, especially in the north of the island. Over the last two centuries Tinos has suffered considerable emigration; but the population, estimated at as high as 25,000 in the mid 19th century, has now stabilised at a little over 8,000 today.

The guide to the island has been divided into three sections

* *Tinos Chora & environs*
* *The east of the island*
* *The west of the island*

TINOS CHORA & ENVIRONS

CHORA

Modern Tinos is a busy, functional centre which has grown up around the island's only reasonable harbour on the west coast and over the site of the ancient, Hellenistic city of *Tenos*. It has been so much rebuilt in recent years that it has lost a lot of the character it must once have possessed. What is left of the old quarter lies directly inland of the port to the northeast. Here two large churches encapsulate an important aspect of the history of the island: within a stone's throw of each other are the Orthodox church of the *Malamatenia* and the Roman Catholic church of St Nicholas, symbolising the historic co-existence on the island of large communities of the two denominations. The columns of the *templon* screen of the *Malamatenia* church exhibit a good variety of polychrome marbles from all over the Aegean. The **fountain** in the main street just west of the two churches, on the other hand, is encased in the native, local grey and white marble of northern Tinos, its waterspouts framed by plaques carved with highly ornate floral designs typical of a '*rococo*' taste which prevailed in late Ottoman times.

The carving was produced nonetheless in the flourishing local marble workshops of Tinos. Behind the fountain is a pleasing neoclassical mansion—one of many in the streets of this area, most of which are now empty, but may, with luck, avoid demolition.

The main harbour mole bears a simple memorial to a defining event of modern Greek and Tiniot history: the destruction by an Italian submarine torpedo of the Greek naval cruiser *Helle*, or *Ἕλλη*, on 15 August 1940. This was the Feast of the Assumption—one of the island's two most important festivals of the sacred calendar. The event was an omen of the imminent outbreak of hostilities between Greece and Italy ten weeks later, and had the effect of electrifying Greek national sentiment. On the promontory which protects the harbour to the south is a monument to the islanders who lost their lives in that war. From it, there is a good view back of the town, of the site of the Hellenistic city which was concentrated mostly to the west of the pilgrimage church, and of the peak of the ancient acropolis at Xoburgo (*see below*), which dominates the scene from above and behind. The impressive building lining the east side of the port now houses the 'Tinos Cultural Centre'—a library and exhibition centre for the island.

A broad boulevard, paved with marble, leads straight

uphill from the port to the Italianate **church of the Panaghia Evangelistria** (the Virgin of the Annunciation)
which dominates the town from above. For the Greek
Orthodox community this is one of the most important
places of pilgrimage in the country. Up the right-hand side
of the street there is a roll of matting which runs the whole
distance (500m) from port to church: this is for those who
wish to make the ascent to the church on their knees, with
feet usually bared and head covered. The traffic of pilgrims seems to flow in tides: on Sundays and feast-days
the crowds in and around the church are daunting; but
all day every day there is a continual flux of worshippers,
pilgrims and faithful, all with a petition to the Virgin. The
living importance of the shrine is moving to witness.

In July 1822 a nun by the name of Pelagia at the monastery of Kechrovouni (*see below*) said she had been visited—
twice in a dream and once in a vision—by the Virgin Mary
who had revealed to her the whereabouts of a miraculous
icon which was buried in the ground just outside the city
of Tinos. In the autumn, excavations—in which the nuns
themselves participated—were begun and uncovered the ruins of a Byzantine church. On 30 January 1823 the icon was
found, and work began on the construction of the church
that stands today. Greeks from inside and outside Greece

sent contributions for the building of the whole complex
and it was completed in 1831. The particular celebrations
of the icon are on the feasts of the Annunciation (25 March)
and the Assumption (15 August).

Curiously, the approaching boulevard is not axial to the
church itself, and runs just off-centre (just as was the case
in many ancient Greek sanctuaries). Before the entrance is
a fine patterned terrace laid in pebbles. The marble fountain between the two main doors is local work, carved in
1828: the Virgin in the scene of the *Annunciation* has a
languor and a richness of costume which is worthy of Tit-
ian. In fact, the influence of Italian style in every element
here is considerable.

The two monumental entrances lead into a paved court,
more grandiose than intimate. The church has two levels:
the upper church houses the icon and is the '*Ano Naos*' (upper sanctuary) for large public ceremonies; below is the
sanctuary of the '*Evresi*', or 'discovery' of the icon. The quality of the **Byzantine chant** here is, in general, particularly
high: visiting the church on a Sunday or a feast-day will en-
sure you get to hear it at its best.

Inside the **Upper Sanctuary**, the **icon** itself is on your left
in an ornate ogival frame—protected in silver sheathing and

so encrusted in ornamentation that the original object of veneration is virtually invisible. It is surrounded by silver *ex voto* pendants: these depict anything from fighter-jets, cots, houses and boats, through to forks or maps of Cyprus. As would be expected, the iconostasis is of massive proportions and complexity—incorporating a fine selection of plaques in various Aegean polychrome marbles, an array of 19th century icons and intricate virtuoso woodwork. All around the gallery of the courtyard, and on the raised section of pavement below, are hundreds of inscriptions and graffiti carved by visitors in the marble. Above the exterior door in the north east corner which leads down into the Baptistery is an older inscription praising the 'Light of Life', probably from the original Byzantine church on the site.

The **Sanctuary of the** *Evresi* below is divided into three parallel chapels, corresponding to the three apses above. Here, in the central one, are the remains of the once buried Byzantine church of St John the Baptist where the icon was found: appropriately, in this and the chapel to the right, are large baptismal fonts in copper lined with tin, and one stone font (for non-Orthodox believers) below a very darkened fresco of the 1820s. The north chapel (to left) contains the spring which appeared at the time of the discovery, now faced with a very worn marble front showing the Virgin Mary as the 'Fount of Life'. This image is picked up in one of the most beautiful icons (immediately to the left of the entrance door) which also shows the Virgin as the *Zoödochos Pigi*, with fine decorations on the depicted fountain and a heterogeneous assembly of beneficiaries below. The theme of the *Zoödochos Pigi*, or Fount of Life, provided continuity (through the symbol of water) with the dedication of the Byzantine Church to the Baptist. The church of the *Evresi* also contains part of the torpedo which destroyed the *Helle*.

As you make towards the exit of the courtyard, a room to the right of the two main gateways contains a **picture gallery** of works by Tiniot and other artists, as well as a miscellany of gifts—ivories, furniture, ceramics (and a stupendous polychrome marble floor-lamp which could have stepped from a painting by Alma-Tadema). The paintings are generally not in good condition, and many need re-stretching and re-lining. The interest principally lies in seeing how deeply 19th century artistic taste in Greece was in thrall to Italian (especially Neapolitan) 17th and 18th century style. Understanding this helps one to realise just how positively Greece has since developed its own very particular artistic idiom in recent times.

Worthy of particular note here are two paintings by Konstantinos Giatras (1811–88)—a finely observed portrait of Capodistrias (*no.13*) and *Mother and Daughter* (*no. 25*); and a study of an *Old Woman Writing* (*no. 54*) by Nikolaos

Gyzis (1842–1901), a native of Tinos and one of Greece's greatest academic painters of the 19th century, who studied and eventually settled in Munich, where he absorbed more deeply than any the spirit of the prevailing narrative, orientalist taste.

Returning to the main boulevard outside and heading towards the port once again, you find, half way down on the right, the island's **Archaeological Museum** (*open 8.30–3, closed Mon*).

The small museum consists of three rooms and a courtyard: the fourth room, to the left of the entrance, is the curator's office, and it is worth asking to see inside (a favour kindly and willingly conceded) because it contains some of the best examples of carved Tiniot window-casements of the 18th and 19th centuries, some of which are decorated with beautiful marine motifs. These constitute one of the most delightful and typical architectural decorations of the island.

On display in the three main rooms are: early finds made at the site of the Archaic *Thesmophoreion*, or sanctuary to Demeter, below Xoburgo; and later finds, both pottery and sculpture, from the Hellenistic town and cemetery of Ancient *Tenos*. The courtyard contains fragmentary sculptures and architectural

members from the sanctuary
of Poseidon and Amphitrite at
Kionia (*see pp. 74–76*), which
are exhibited in the peristyle,
around a late Roman mosaic
floor. The museum also contains some explanatory material on excavations currently
in progress on the island.

Two exhibits deserve
special mention: the magnifi-
cently decorated *7th century
BC funerary *pithoi* from the
sanctuary below Xoburgo,
made from a remark-
ably crimson-coloured clay.
The scenes of hunting and
mythology—full of vigour
and confident draughtsman-
ship—depicted on these huge
urns are picked out in clear
relief, and then enhanced
and decorated with a sharp
tool. The strangeness of the
figures of deities with wings,
primitive faces and unfamiliar
dress, reminds us how little
we understand of the im-
aginative world of this period
which stood, after all, on the
threshold of the Archaic and
Classical Age.

At the other end of the
spectrum is a creation of the
Hellenistic enlightenment,
the **1st century BC sundial** or
clock, attributed to Androni-
cus Kyrrhestes, the ingen-
ious creator of the beautiful
Horologium in the *agora* of
Athens, known commonly as
the 'Tower of the Winds'. The
precisely-carved and meas-
ured-out declivity in the top
of the single block of marble
held a vertical bronze needle
on the outside edge; this cast
the shadow across the grid of
calibrated lines in the bowl
towards the inside edge, which

was decorated with a (still partially visible) face of Helios. The measurements on the exterior would seem to suggest that this was only one part of a larger horological complex.

THE ENVIRONS OF CHORA

North

The construction of a new ring-road around the city has brought to light (just north of the Evangelistria Church) stretches of the **walls of the 4th century BC town**, and the **base of a bastion**. Where it passes to the east of the Evangelistria Church, the work has revealed an **ancient cemetery** and the **foundations of an ancient round tower** which would have had good visibility and sight lines to another tower (foundations only) on the hill of Kato Kastri to the west of the town.

East

Two and half kilometres east of Chora, the coast road passes a conspicuous conical promontory to the seaward side: this is **Vryo Kastro**, crowned by the site of Tinos's earliest prehistoric settlement. Ascent is easy and the views are good, but there is little for the visitor to see, beyond the interesting site itself and the quantity of potsherds under foot—some even from large *amphorae* and tiles, indicat-

ing a continuity of habitation well into later historic epochs. The first settlement here, taking advantage of natural defences, a panoramic position and the proximity of
two natural harbours appears to have been in the Early
Bronze Age (early 3rd millennium BC). Vryo Kastro was
linked by marine trade routes with sites of the same epoch
such as Aghia Irini on Kea and Akrotiri on Thera, but has
yielded a lesser wealth of artefacts than they have.

West

Three kilometres west of Chora, the coast road passes
the site of the 4th century BC **sanctuary of Poseidon and
Amphitrite** (*open 8.30–3, closed Mon*). In ancient times
this important and busy sanctuary was linked to the city
of *Tenos* by a sacred way, which passed through the city's
cemeteries. At first glance the site looks unpromising, but
with the help of imagination it soon comes to life. Strabo
was impressed by the multitudes who came to celebrate
the *Poseidonia* festivals here; he comments that the sanctuary was '…θέας ἄξιον', 'something worth seeing' (*Geog.*,
X 5, 11)—more interesting, by implication, than the city
itself. The probable reason for the choice of site lies in its
northwest corner, where a spring (now dry) would have
given rise in earliest times to a dense stand of trees or
'sacred grove'.

In front, and to the left on entering, lies the podium of the **temple**. Nothing of the superstructure is standing, although some column drums in grey marble at the western end have been erected where they fell, rather than where they originally stood. To the south (between the temple and the sea) is the base of another small temple or shrine which, in its clearly cut base-course of finely dressed marble, shows several signs of where the bronze dowels and staples which held the marble pieces together have been lifted and removed. Further behind this, in the southwest corner, are the remains of Roman **baths** which were added later: the red, water-proofed plaster of one of the chambers is still well preserved.

The water for these baths came from the spring and *nymphaeum* in the northwest corner, which is the most interesting building here. In the centre is a semicircular stone bench where, in the shade of the roof supported by the columns in front (bases visible), people could sit and enjoy the cool. On either side were two rectangular basins of water, constantly filled by a jet of water channelled through two grooves in the marble above. The plan of these two tanks is visible (note column bases) and some of the grooved vertical slabs which closed the spaces between the columns are also recognisable, especially on the left. This provided a beautiful setting and the constant sound of running water for visitors. To the rear of the structure, it is possible to see how the water is led from the main spring down a covered channel on the left (west) side into the narrow retaining tanks behind the seats, from where it flows out into the two open, lower tanks.

In the opposite corner, at the back of the area, is a semi-circular **honorific or sacred monument**. It was once crowned with a ring of statuary (the foot-fixtures in one of the blocks are still visible). The much eroded inscription behind mentions near its centre '….[*Posei*]…*don kai Amphitriti*'. Visible at the far southeast corner is the end of a long stoa which then extends much further to the east. Given that the distance from the outside line of columns (north row) to the doorsteps of the buildings behind (south line) is approximately five metres, the stoa must have been very long, if it were to possess customary proportions. The large area between the stoa and the temple was an open court paved in marble—in aspect, probably not that different from the one at the Church of the Evangelistria.

THE EAST OF THE ISLAND

Walking on Tinos. The next two sections suggest an itinerary which can easily be accomplished by car, and many parts of which can be followed by using public transport. Tinos, however, is well organised for walkers and a network of (partially) signposted footpaths and mule-tracks crisscrosses the island. This, combined with the natural beauty of the landscape, makes walking here a joy. A small useful publication which is available in bookshops in the Chora and entitled 'A Travelogue of Tinos', explains relatively clearly a number of recommendable walks across the island.

THE SOUTHEAST OF THE ISLAND & THE KECHROVOUNI CONVENT

The road which heads due east from Chora goes towards Ormos Aghiou Ioannou Porto and the sandy beaches which look across to Mykonos from the southeast corner of the island. Exactly 1km after the attractive church of Aghia Barbara (which is on your left after 4km from Tinos), the **Hellenistic tower** of Movolo is visible in the field below and to the right. Although truncated and not as massive, this is similar in concept to the tower of Aghios Petros on Andros (*see pp. 48–52*). Again, as at Aghios Petros, there are four curious, indented grooves (approx. 10cm wide) running vertically down the stonework. No entrance is visible, but this may have been covered by the accumulation of soil around the base. There is a broken floor over a lower chamber at the foot of the tower which would otherwise be inaccessible if there were no door.

Returning to Aghia Barbara, a road to the north leads up towards the villages of the interior: first Triandaros, then Dio Choriá, Mountados, etc. It is worth stopping at **Dio Choriá** for the simple beauty of the village. Some way above the fountains by the road are two more springs in the main *plateia*. The centre of the village is an irregular and beautiful amphitheatre of buildings with a shaded washing area, marble paving, plants, and the shade of plane trees. There are many covered and arcaded streets that wind between the houses.

Two kilometres beyond Dio Choriá, the road passes the **nunnery of Kechrovouni** (*closed 1–4.30*), dedicated to the *Koimisis tis Theotokou* (Dormition of the Virgin). It was here in July 1822 that one of the nuns, Sister (Saint) Pelagia, who was canonised in 1971, had her dreams and her vision of the Virgin Mary which were to change the course of the island's history. The nunnery is more like a fortified Cycladic village than a nunnery—a labyrinth of tiny alleys and houses. It thrives today, and has always had a large community of nuns. The foundation is of the 12th century; but visible today are mostly buildings of the 18th century and after. The oldest part of the complex is the tiny chapel of the *Zoödochos Pigi*, standing just in front and to the left of the entrance to the main *catholicon*. It is a single chamber, roofed in irregular schist blocks which are supported on small and irregular beams of vine-wood. There is no iconostasis but there are blackened icons painted on the wall instead. The *catholicon* of the nunnery, by contrast, has fine stalls carved in walnut wood and a particularly ornate iconostasis. Most moving of all are Sister Pelagia's tiny quarters (*above and to the right of the catholicon*) which are of an exemplary and pious simplicity: a living room, a tiny kitchen with a stove and a few pots, and a bedroom with a minuscule bed and stone pillow. Near to her abode is the newly rebuilt church of the *Taxiarches*, or Archangels, in dazzling and decorated white marble—all cut by machine and consequently somewhat dead to the touch and to the eye.

The views from Kechrovouni (when it is not in the clouds) are excellent. To the north, beyond the monastery, the road drops a little into the interior of the island. All around is an intricate patchwork of terracing, representing the monumental labour of centuries which was aimed at creating cultivable fields out of the barren hillsides and stemming the erosion of the soil. There is a grandeur and an openness to the landscape. To the east rises **Mount Tsikniás** (729m), rocky and barren, where at least one mythological tradition sited the abode of Aeolos, god of the winds. Here alone no attempt has been made to terrace the arid slopes and they have been left wild. They are home to the rare and endemic, yellow *Alyssum tenium*.

Below the mountain lies **Stení**. This is another beautiful village, but quite different in feel from Dio Choriá. The main street runs beneath arches; there are plane trees, gardens and springs. The village has a small Folklore Museum (*open mornings in July and August only*) containing the typical objects and furniture of a Tiniot house over the last 200 years.

AROUND XOBURGO

Almost 2km due west of Stení, the road passes a junction where a track leads (left) up to the Jesuit pilgrimage church of the Sacred Heart, and towards the dramatic summit of *[E]xoburgo above it. 'Xoburgo' (sometimes transliterated 'Exomburgo', or just 'Xomburgo') simply means the 'settlement' (*burgo*) 'outside' (*exo*): this refers to the fact that the area outside of the castle and around the summit of the hill was densely inhabited during the Middle Ages. Today we only see the remains of the fortified castle on the peak which was the protection and nerve-centre of the community. Of the town itself, very little remains: just the two fine, vaulted cisterns (fed by a spring and still in use) at the point where the concrete track to the church joins the asphalt road: another water fountain lies just below and to the south of the road, about 50m back towards the east. The only other remnants are the massive ruins of a **monumental gate** just below the church. The huge dimensions of this once arched space—which was not without decorative elements as the columns on the ground bear witness—must have constituted an impressive entrance to the town and castle. The **Venetian fortress keep** is reached up a steep, stony path from the church. Though expanded in later centuries, the first construction here was probably made in the 13th century by the Ghisi family, who were the island's first Venetian overlords. The outer enceinte is beautifully constructed and still standing in part, in spite of the dismantling of the fortress in 1715 by the Turks. To the right you pass a cistern, still relatively well preserved. At the summit, two bastions dominate and control the final switchback of the ascent, through an outer and then an inner gate. Here the masonry is of finer workmanship. The site has survived much better than Apano Kastro on Andros, which can be seen to the northwest from here. The *views from the top (in spite of a forest of telecommunications antennae and other electronic instruments of torture) are wonderful. The islands are laid out across the sea like plates on a dinner-table—with Delos appearing unexpectedly small.

From the Sacred Heart church a path below leads down to the north, between stone walls, to the delightful village of **Koumáros** (0.6km) whose courtyards and streets without traffic become an animated open air salon of activity in the evenings.

Also from the Sacred Heart church, but in the opposite direction, a path leads down (past the chapel of Aghia Eleni) towards Xinára, and skirts the south side of the Xoburgo hill. This brings you after 10–15 minutes to the small but interesting area of the remains of **Ancient Tenos** and its lower acropolis of the Geometric, Archaic and Classical periods. As you descend, you first come upon a row of foundations of 6th century BC buildings to the left of the path; then, just below, a section of massive, polygonal Archaic walling. This defensive enceinte, which defined the lower extent of the Archaic acropolis, continues to the right of the path towards the west and north, enclosing a large apron-shaped area and rising up steeply to engage with the face of the south precipice of the mountain above. At one point it cuts abruptly across an area which has recently been excavated; this has revealed some earlier (Geometric period) wall-foundations and a very precisely bordered rectangular hearth which lies partly under the Archaic walls. Further west are more walls describing a rectangular form outside of the enceinte: these probably represent a later re-use of Archaic material. The structure has been recently identified as a *Thesmophoreion* or **sanctuary of Demeter**. Above this, and once again well within the enceinte, are more foundations with storage *pithoi* still in place. It is from this area that the magnificent decorated *pithoi* in the island's Archaeological Museum come.

VOLAX & THE CENTRAL NORTH OF THE ISLAND

Returning to the asphalt road and continuing towards the north and west, the landscape suddenly begins to change: the fields and terracing stop and a dramatic landscape of curious, rounded boulders abruptly takes their place. This is the *valley of Volax—a tiny village which sits alone, like a white beacon, in the middle of this foreboding, lunar landscape. (*Detour of 1.4km to right at junction.*) The isolated settlement (which is a predominantly Catholic community) grew up here because of the presence of the strong spring just below. Perhaps a little too picturesque for its own good today, it is nonetheless an unforgetta-ble assemblage of varied stone-houses and flowering gar-dens, where the traditional local skill of basket-weaving still flourishes. There is also a pleasant taverna.

No other landscape in the Greek islands is quite the same as this strange and circumscribed area where either a volcanic eruption or meteorite fall, many millions of years ago, littered the surface of the earth with these large bomb-like boulders of granite. They look for all the world like gigantic, black hailstones; and in fact their presence here—seeming like something hurled by an angry and powerful god of the elements—may explain the tradition which located the abode of Aeolos, god of the winds, on the top of nearby Mount Tsikniás.

Just before Skaládos, the landscape quickly returns to normal once again and, at the village of Krókos, the road descends into the broad valley that divides the north of the island into two. Here the elaborate *dovecotes that have been evident sporadically up until now become much more numerous—some in plain stone, but the ma-jority whitewashed.

THE DOVECOTES OF TINOS

Perhaps over a thousand dovecotes are still standing in the valleys and hillsides of Tinos—each one different and each an outburst of architectural fantasy whose decorative value often far exceeds any functional need. These small free-standing avian palaces are the most memorable characteristic of the island's landscape; they blend into it as though they were some kind of rare tree. The breeding of doves can be dated and accounted for historically on the island; but the remarkable originality and quantity of these tiny buildings can in the end only be explained by an exceptional creativity on the part of the islanders—further propelled and sharpened by the forces of fashion and of competition to outdo others.

Domesticated doves came to Greece from Mesopotamia, brought by the 'enemy' during the Persian wars. As the sacred bird of Astarte and Aphrodite (both divinities of love) and later as the purveyor of peace and the Holy Spirit in Christian imagery, doves have always been imbued with important symbolism. But they have also had more banal and practical uses—namely providing food, fertilizer, methods of

communication, and as objects for target practice. In
the Aegean, they were commonly released from boats
long before arrival at a port in order to announce the
return of mariners and cargos. On Tinos, an island
where almost every acre of land was painstakingly
given over to cultivation and where in consequence
there was no pasture for flocks and herds, meat was
very scarce and the dove provided a compact and
valuable source of protein. An average sized dovecote
with a hundred breeeding pairs could provide nearly
200kg of meat annually. The birds' droppings fur-
thermore were a valuable fertilizer for the poor soil
of the island, and could also be used as an ingredient
in the making of a natural explosive.

The practice of intensive breeding and husband-
ing of doves may have been introduced to Tinos by
the Venetians in the 13th century: we know that Tiniot squabs, pickled in oil and vinegar, were a popular delicacy in Constantinople and Smyrna in the
late Middle Ages. But the first notices (in wills and
visitors' accounts) that we have of the dovecote as
an architectural entity are only from the 18th century, at a time when Venetian rule gave way to Ot-

toman occupation. Under Ottoman rule many of the Aegean islands became more prosperous and there was greater freedom of movement for persons and goods. With increasing wealth, it seems that the dovecote became a kind of status symbol and just as the villages competed with one another to raise finer churches and bell-towers than their neighbours', individuals competed with one another in the building of more elaborate dovecotes.

The dovecotes are clustered mostly in the sheltered valleys of the island and are situated never far from fresh water. They face away from the prevailing north wind and are generally of modest dimensions (e.g. 3 x 4 x 5m). They possess often more than one floor within: this meant they could be used also for storage, and even for accommodation in the busy periods of the agricultural calendar. The most important element was the lattice of openings at the top and the external shelves on the sunny sides for the birds to bask on. The openings were created in fine geometric patterns with small slates mounted in triangles, sunbursts and diamond shapes: it is here that the fantasy of the builders acquires its own momentum, creat-

ing purely decorative patterns all around the building well beyond the number of openings which the
birds themselves required.

The road descends, passing a junction (to right) for Skla-
vochóri (the village where the Tiniot painter, Nikos Gyzis,
was born): it then levels out in a broad and fertile alluvial
valley which runs to the sea at **Kolymbíthra**. There are a
couple beaches in the attractive inlet here—beautiful and
peaceful, but with little shade. Returning 3.5km inland
to the junction at Komi and continuing straight on for
2km brings you to Kato Klisma. A junction here leads to
the wild, north side of the western end of the island (*see
below*).

THE WEST OF THE ISLAND

This itinerary begins at Kato Klisma, where the previous itinerary ends. To reach this point directly from Chora (15.5km), take the main Pyrgos/Panormos road north. At the main junction at 5.5km, follow the road to the left and west (the road to the right leads towards Krokos, passing Xinara, an interesting village dominated by the Roman Catholic Diocesan Church). At the next junction, after a further 1.4km, a road leads off down to Smardaki, a valley densely and picturesquely scattered with dovecotes. By turning right at the subsequent junction (after another 3.5km), you come to Kato Klisma again (5km).

From Kato Klisma a road leads uphill to **Aetofoliá** (literally 'eagle's nest') and the north of the island. Aetofoliá is rich in springs which rise at the upper end of the main street: the street soon becomes a mule-path as it heads out of the village, and leads to a charming stone bridge in the gorge and then up to the wild plateau above. The newly built asphalt road rises by a different route to the same point.

The northern slopes of Tinos are barren, wild and precipitous; but the landscape is everywhere punctuated with walls, deserted habitations, and the ubiquitous evidence of the attempts of man to work the land wherever possible. Apparently in the middle of nowhere, you come upon the base of a square **Hellenistic tower** once again, and a section of ancient wall nearby. (*It is not easy to find this site; it is best to take as orientation point the right hand turn-off marked 'Aghii Anargyri and Agios Panteliemon' which is 4.8km from the Kato Klisma junction. Back-tracking (in the direction of Aetofoliá) 500m, on the turn of the third bend—before reaching a new house and church on the right—is a low stone building. Crossing the wall here and descending past the two stone buildings, you find the tower after about 75m, with the segment of walling just a little further on and below.*) The base of the tower is constructed in masonry that has been finely dressed, in the customary manner of the 4th and 3rd centuries BC; the wall is more difficult to date because it has been added to with small stones, in recent epochs, both above and at the ends. The site is remote and the tower is positioned oddly with no clear sight-lines to other visible towers along the coast: nor does the area show signs of ancient mining or intensive cultivation. Most probably it was an isolated garrison-post and watch-tower, surveying the waters to the north of the island.

The Aetofoliá to Isternia road continues through

a rocky landscape with wide views of the sea; it passes the 18th century monastery of the Panaghia Katapolianí (currently undergoing extensive restoration) and rejoins (13km) the main Chora to Pyrgos road which runs up the southern coast of the island, just above Isternia. On the windy and exposed saddle above (to south) are the ruins of several **windmills**, and, beside the junction, a decidedly odd church built in the last century with a bell-tower that looks like a cross between a dovecote and a lighthouse.

PYRGOS

Pyrgos (formerly 'Pánormos') is the largest village on the island, situated on the south side of the wide valley which runs down to the sea at Ormos Panórmou, the island's only natural, deep anchorage. The road to Pyrgos from Istérnia passes numerous small quarries: at first they are of a white and a pale green marble; then further north, of a darker and more uniformly grey marble. Stone quarrying, cutting and sculpting has always been the principal activity in this part of Tinos. The history of Pyrgos is intimately linked to the working of stone, and every street, building and square is paved or constructed or embellished with it: signs, covers for electricity meters, even the bus shelter, are all made from white marble.

The village straddles two sides of a shallow gorge. Life centres on the enchanting *plateia* with its cafés and tavernas grouped around a 150 year-old plane tree and facing the fine marble water-fountain. For those who have the fortune to be in Pyrgos at Easter-time, this square is home to an unforgettable Holy Saturday procession with all its attendant liturgical drama, social complexity, and exquisite sweetmeats: towards midnight, the resplendently decorated and competing *epitaphioi* from the various churches of the village, each with their own chanting processions, converge on this tiny space in what is one of the finest Easter spectacles in the Cyclades.

The square's **marble water-fountain** was first built in 1784 and its back wall remains that of the original 18th century construction: the front arcade with the large inscribed urn in the centre was added in 1929 however. The village's more functional washing-house is located about 20m down the street to the east.

North and west of the square are a couple of small **museums** and an exhibition space, which celebrate one of the most famous artists who hailed from Pyrgos: the sculptor **Giannoúlis Chalepás** (1851–1938). The museums (*open daily 11.30–2, 6–8*) are side by side. The first is a tiny academy building which houses a number of casts as well as the artists' models made by Chalepas and Dimitris Phillipotes. (These still have their points attached for three-point copying. This is because stone sculptors—with the notable exception of a very few, such as Michelangelo and Bernini—never 'create' directly into the marble, but prepare their works first in a full-size model in plaster or clay, and then transfer them, by the mechanical process of three-point copying, into stone.) There is also a series of fine portrait busts. Chalepas is the principal focus of this collection; and his workshop and house are preserved in the building next door, which constitutes the second museum. It also gives a good idea of what a typical Tiniot house, in the early part of the last century, would have been like. The simple rooms are strangely reminiscent of those painted by Chalepas's contemporary, van Gogh.

Like van Gogh, Chalepas suffered long bouts of mental illness. At a very early age he showed extraordinary talent in stone-cutting. He studied in Athens at the Academy of Fine Arts, but in his late 20s he began to suffer mental instability which culminated in a nervous breakdown at the age of 27, not long after he had completed one of his most remarkable and renowned works, the so-called 'Sleeping Lady'—a funerary memorial to Sophia Aphentaki for the cemetery in Athens. His illness led him to destroy many of his own works and to attempt suicide. He was confined to a mental institu-

tion in Corfu for over 12 years, before returning to Pyrgos
on Tinos in the care of his mother. Only after her death in
1916 was he able once again, at the age of 65, to produce
sculpture freely; he continued for the remaining 20 years of
his life, urged on by a sense of lost time, to produce remarkable work and to earn a reputation as one of the foremost
sculptors of modern Greece.

Pyrgos is also the birthplace of one of the most important Greek painters of the late 19th century, **Nikephoros
Lytras** (1832–1904). Like his friend and contemporary
from Tinos, Nikolaos Gyzis, Lytras studied in Munich,
favoured by the strong links at that time between Bavaria
and Othonian Greece. He was primarily a genre painter
of anecdotal and historical scenes, whose paintings possessed a remarkable luminosity of finish. Nikolaos Lytras
(1883–1927) and Perikles Lytras (1888–1940), also successful painters, were his sons. Their works are sometimes
exhibited in the third and last element of the museum-
group in Pyrgos: returning towards the centre of the village and to the main street, it is the first building with a
colonnade which you encounter.

In 2008 the new **Museum of Marble Crafts of Tinos**
(*open daily year round, except Tues, 10–6 pm in summer,
10–5 pm in winter*) was opened to the public. The large

compound of state-of-the-art buildings and exhibition spaces dominates the village from its northeast edge. It is a museum of considerable interest, although the experience of visiting it is at the opposite end of the spectrum from that given by the little house and studio of Chalepas.

The permanent exhibition is dedicated to the quarrying, technology and craftsmanship of marble in the 19th and 20th centuries, and explains the successive processes of extraction, preparation, working and finishing of marble objects, from start to finish, with exemplary clarity. The greatest emphasis is on the tools, machines and techniques involved; the marble works exhibited are mostly ecclesiastical, funerary or domestic pieces of recent production. There is also a fine collection of pattern-drawings and designs for marble objects. In Pyrgos the working of marble, which was once a village craft practised by families of artesans, has been supercharged into a production of industrial scale. Even if the museum, in its size and grandiosity, tends to glorify that evolution, the experience of visiting its displays and the information which they impart should not be missed.

THE WESTERN TIP OF TINOS

From Pyrgos a road leads west to the village of Marlás. Just before entering the village you pass on the left a small quarry, which is now out of use. Here, in the upper area is the rarer green marble of Tinos. Beyond **Marlás**, the un-made road to Koumelás, descends into a landscape which is barren, but nonetheless meticulously terraced for a cultivation which has now almost completely ceased. At a turn in the road after 3km, a view opens down into the massive quarries of pure grey marble far below. They are still being actively exploited, and their vast, smoothly facetted sides dwarf the people and machinery working within them. Going east from Marlás, after 2km the asphalt road ends at the church of Aghia Thekla and, just below, the small monastery of Kirá Xéni ('Lady of the Strangers'). Between these two (beside the road above the car parking area) are the partial remains of a care-fully fashioned, **Mycenaean bee-hive tomb**, dated by the pottery found in it to the 14th century BC. Only half of the small dome survives, and it has been considerably filled in. When complete it would probably have been ap-proached by a *dromos*, or entry passage, opening to the east and facing towards the rising sun over Panormos Bay which lies below.

ISTERNIA AND SOUTH TO CHORA

On the main south coast road which returns towards
Chora once again there are a couple of points of particular interest in addition to the fine views to south and west.
The village of **Isternia** has the most panoramic site of any
village on the island. Its winding main street beetles along
a ledge below the summit of Mount Prasa (616m). Like
Pyrgos, this is a village which has lived on the quarrying,
cutting and carving of marble, and every element of the
construction and decoration of the buildings bears witness to that fact. Eleven kilometres beyond Isternia and
13km from Chora, just below the road to the seaward
side, is the base of the square, **Hellenistic tower** at Av-
dos, which stands today to a height of approximately 4m,
constructed of regular 40cm courses of rusticated marble. The tower clearly functioned as a signalling and look-
out post. Once again it bears the lightly indented vertical
band in its exterior stonework which was noted also on
the tower at Movolo on Tinos (*pp. 77–78*) and of Aghios
Petros on Andros (*pp. 48–52*): here the band runs down
the outside of the northwest corner of the building.

A half-kilometre beyond the tower, to the landward
side of the road, is a fascinating object of geological interest: an oddly hollowed out **boulder of plutonic rock**,

which shows remarkable evidence of both physical and chemical erosion. The piece of rock, which is roughly spherical with a diameter of about 2.5m, by its extensive erosion gives us a fascinating picture of the inside of these strange volcanic 'cannon-balls'. The undulating striations of the interior are rich in minerals (copper, iron, manganese etc.), which have given them their very different colours. Exposure to chemical elements present in the atmosphere has increased this effect and has pock-marked the surface of the interior, which was first exposed to the elements by the breaching of its exterior 'shell' by the physical erosion of wind and water. Such curious formations are the result of a slow cooling process which occurs deep down near a volcano's reservoir of lava: the closer the liquid rock is to the volcanic focus, the greater the temperature and the slower the process of cooling—which may be prolonged for hundreds or thousands of years. Crystals therefore have ample time to form. Because of the heavy pressure on top, steam cannot expand and escape, but will remain in millions of infinitely tiny cavities inside the rock: these give rise to the surface visible here in the interior of the boulder. When there is a subsequent cataclysm, this plutonic rock, which still may not have solidified, is disturbed and ejected up through cooler material: in the process it will solidify in the form of the round boulders we see here.

The coast road, running southeast high above the shore, returns after a further 11.5km to the capital of the island once again.

PRACTICAL INFORMATION

842 00 **Tinos**: area 197 sq.km; perimeter 114km; resident population 8,115; max. altitude 729m. **Port Authorities**: T. 22830 22220. **Travel and information**: **Windmills Travel**, T. 22830 23398, fax. 23327, www. tinos-tinos.com

ACCESS

Access to the island, which has no airport, is from the Attic port of Rafina by two, twice daily services—by regular (3½ hrs) and high-speed (1½ hrs) ferries. Boats only call at Tinos Chora, the island's capital.

LODGING

Most of the island's hotels are in Tinos Chora, and along the beaches to east and west of the town; good rooms for rent in private houses can also be found in Pyrgos, and in the villages all over the island. The **Hotel Tinion** in Chora is quiet, comfortable and architecturally pleasing, and lies a little to the east of the main port area (*open Apr–Oct: T. 22830 22261, fax: 24754*). Simple, reasonably priced, hospitable and well-appointed, overlooking the harbour yet far enough away to be peaceful, is the **Voreades Hotel**, named after the sons of the cooling North wind (*open Mar–Nov: T. 22830 23845; www.voreades.gr*). If you have your own transportation, then the best solution on the island is the delightful *Victoria Drouga's Rooms*—one of the most pleasing and reasonable places to stay in the Cyclades both for its beautiful position on Kolymbithra Bay and for the quality of its food and breakfasts (*T. 22830 51309, fax 51729, www.tinos-victoria. com*).

EATING

The **Taverna Victoria**, attached to the small hotel on Kolymbithra Bay (*see above under lodging*) serves excellent island specialties in a lovely setting. Chora itself has no shortage of tavernas, but none particularly stands out: for good local food it is generally best to eat in the surrounding villages, some of which are only a few minutes by car or taxi from the main town. The taverna, **Ta Lefkes** at Triandaros (6km—with springs and good views) is a good place to sample the piquant, local Tiniot sausage, fresh *myzithra* cheese, and other local dishes. *Maratho-tiganita* is a very delicious local dish served in many village tavernas—a kind of vegetable fritter, flavoured with both dried and fresh fennel. Surprisingly, given the number of dovecotes, it is not easy to find squab on the menu; the tavernas in Krókos and Loutrá and around the valley below are those that most commonly serve it.

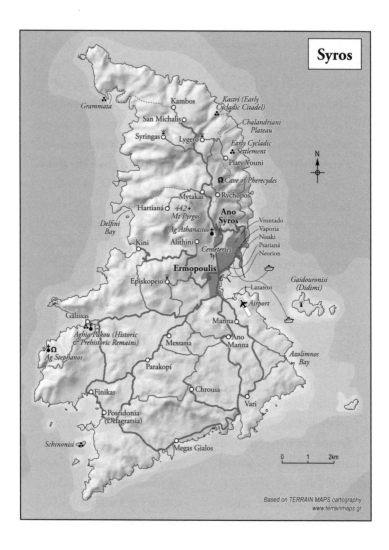

Syros

Grammata

Kambos

Kastrí (Early Cycladic Citadel)

San Michalis

Chalandriani Plateau

Syringas   Lygero

Early Cycladic Settlement

Platy Vouni

N

Ω *Cave of Pherecydes*

Mytakas   Rychopos

Hartianá   442 ◆

Mt Pyrgos   **Ano Syros**

Delfini Bay   Vrontado
                Vaporia
Ag Athanasios   Nisaki
Kini   Alithini   Psarianá
                Neorion
        Cemeteries
        †

Ermopoulis

Episkopeio   *Gaidouronisi (Didimi)*

        Lazareto

        ✈ *Airport*

Galissas

Aghia Pakou (Historic & Prehistoric Remains)   Manna

        Messaria   Ano Manna

Ω

Ag Stephanos   *Azolimnos Bay*

        Parakopí

Finikas   Chrousa

Poseidonia
(Delagratsia)   Vari

Schinonisi

        Megas Gialos

0   1   2km

Based on TERRAIN MAPS cartography
www.terrainmaps.gr

SYROS

Syros has a feel quite different from the other Cycladic islands. The spacious, marble-surfaced elegance of its Neoclassical port, Ermoupolis, is in vivid contrast to the usual labyrinthine streets and low houses of a Cycladic *chora*. There is an unexpected buzz of activity and urban commerce on Syros. Ermoupolis is the only true city in the Cyclades. Its impressive architecture was the result of wealth generated by a vigorous activity of commerce and shipping in the 19th century, most of which was built up out of utter destitution by refugees fleeing the Turkish destructions of Chios and Psara. The resurgence of optimism and prosperity which Ermoupolis represents is a testimony to the irrepressible enterprise of the Aegean islanders and to their innate *εμπορικό πνεύμα*, or 'genius for commerce'. It is true that the edges of the city today are tinged with the melancholy of a deceased industrial prowess; but the energy is by no means gone, and Ermoupolis remains a stimulating town in which to walk, explore, eat well, listen to the rich heritage of its *rebetiko* music, or simply be a *flâneur*. Outside the city's centre other appealing visits can be made: the tranquil mediaeval settlement of Ano Syros; and the elegiac beauty of the

Orthodox cemetery, with its splendid funerary sculptures set among cypress and palm trees.

Syros is small, and the milder landscape of the island's southern half, has inevitably been conditioned by the prosperity emanating from the port: the land is wherever possible cultivated, inhabited, and dotted with the rural estates of the city's rich. The attractive bays of the island's west coast have become flourishing resorts—the most remarkable of which is the 19th century settlement of Delagratsia (now called Poseidonia), with its eccentric, turreted villas and parks, built competitively by the important families of Ermoupolis. But for those with nostalgia for Cycladic wilderness, the steep and rocky north of the island is in utter contrast to everything else. Dramatic, panoramic and largely uninhabited but for remote clusters of houses, the north seems a world away from the port. It is in this wild and uncompromising setting that the first Early Bronze Age settlements were found by Christos Tsoundas at the end of the 19th century. The artistic creativity of their artefacts and the organisation of their settlements, led him to talk for the first time about a 'Cycladic civilisation'. The citadel of Kastri, dating from the 3rd millennium BC, with its walls, bastions, streets and houses is impressive not merely for the specialist.

At the island's northernmost point, one hour's walk

from where the road ends, is the remote promontory of Grammata, named from the dozens of votive inscriptions—mostly Ancient, but some Byzantine or Mediaeval—scratched on the rocks by mariners who took refuge from storms in this unusually sheltered bay, thanking one divinity for deliverance or invoking another for protection on a voyage. Some are hurried; some meticulously etched and framed; others rudimentarily illustrated. They are one of the strangest and most evocative ancient sights in the Cyclades.

HISTORY

Recent archaeological surveys have identified three Neolithic sites from the 5th millennium BC on Syros in the southern half of the island (at Talanta, at Atsiganokastro near Finikas, and on the east side of the bay of Vari). The strategic location of the island on important maritime routes gave rise to prosperous centres on Syros in the Early Bronze Age, this time in the north of the island—the most famous and remarkable of which is the fortified citadel at Kastrí in the north, which directly superseded the older (Early Cycladic II) settlement nearby at Chalandrianí, in c. 2300 BC. The importance and variety of the artefacts from these two sites have led to one of the main periods and types of Early Cycladic culture being named after the island.

Eumaeus, in Book XV (403 ff) of the *Odyssey* speaks of his island homeland, '*Syríe*', not far from *Ortygia* (Delos); his description of it as fertile, rich in wine and cattle, and abundant in wheat, seems markedly different from the often infertile and rocky island we see today. We hear little of the island in historical antiquity, except that it was the birthplace in the early 6th century BC of Pherecydes, one of the earliest philosophers of the Greek world, who is cited by Diogenes Laertius as possibly the mentor of Pythagoras.

Syros was captured by Samians in the 6th century BC. It allied with the Persians during the Persian wars, but subsequently participated in the First and Second Athenian Leagues. Very little physically remains of the ancient city of *Syros* beyond vestiges visible in the area of Psariana just west of the harbour. Recent archaeological work, however, has uncovered a substantial settlement of the Archaic and Classical periods to the south of Galissas, on the west coast of the island. The (mostly Hellenistic) coinage of *Syros* displays images of the cult of the Cabiri, whose sanctuary has been provisionally identified near the village of Alithini, in the hills to the northwest of the port.

Throughout the Middle Ages the island was known by the name '*Souda*'. Following its inclusion in the Duchy of Naxos, created by Marco Sanudo in the aftermath of the taking of Constantinople in the Fourth Crusade of 1204, a Venetian and Genoese population settled on Syros, on the steep hill to the northwest of the harbour—today's Ano Syros. This gave rise to a Roman Catholic population which predominated on the island well into the 19th century, and survives today as an appreciable proportion of the total number of islanders. In 1633 Capuchin monks settled on the island; in 1640 the island appealed directly to the French king, Louis XIII, for protection against the Turks; and in the early 18th century a Jesuit community also established itself in Ano Syros. This brought to the island precious cultural links with mainstream Europe. Syros had been taken in 1537 by Khaireddin Barbarossa for the Ottoman Sultan, and concessions negotiated with Sultan Murat III in 1579 allowed it some measure of autonomy. Further privileges were accorded in 1779 when, after the occupation of the island by Russians during the First Russo-Turkish War, Syros and Andros were given by Sultan Abdul Hamid I to his favourite niece, Sah Sultana. The freedom and autonomy the two islands subsequently enjoyed allowed them to build merchant fleets and to increase their importance as maritime commercial centres. For this reason Syros was anxious to remain neutral at the time of the outbreak of the Greek War of Independence in 1821. Its neutrality attracted and afforded protection to refugees from other parts of the Greek world who had been dispossessed.

The 19th and 20th century history of Syros is marked by its absorption of large populations of refugees: in 1822

and 1824 from Chios and Psará respectively, after the
Turkish devastations in the Northeastern Aegean; in 1866
from Crete; and in 1923 from Asia Minor, with the 'ex-
change of populations' between Turkey and Greece. The
first refugees, from Chios and Psará, founded and planned
the new city of Ermoupolis around the port, and built it
into the premier industrial centre of Greece and the second city in importance after Athens (which it exceeded
in productivity even so). With the wealth generated from
commerce and shipping, the city was embellished with
fine, marble residences, churches and public buildings
in the second half of the 19th century. Ermoupolis was
a planned neoclassical city, and its inhabitants were Orthodox, in contrast to the traditional, mediaeval 'kastro'
of Ano Syros (Upper, or Old, Syros) which was home to
the Roman Catholic community. In the late 19th century,
the rising importance of the port of Piraeus and the decline in demand for wooden boats and sail-ships dealt a
double blow to the fortunes of Ermoupolis: it responded
by adapting and moving into industrial production instead—of leather, iron, and of cotton especially, thanks to
its close ties to Manchester. But the beginning of the 20th
century saw the erosion of these industries through their

transference to Athens and Piraeus: the last and largest factories were closed by the mid-1930s.

Syros was occupied by the Italians in 1941, and by the Germans from 1943; it was badly bombarded in 1944. After the War it lost 20 per cent of its population through emigration. Since 1980, though, the island has adapted rapidly to new economic reality. After a brief closure, the shipyards—symbolically, the island's most important employer—re-opened in 1994, and now thrive; small industries have returned and tourism (predominantly domestic) now supplements a hesitantly growing economy.

The guide to the island has been divided into three sections:
- *Ermoupolis and Ano Syros*
- *The south of the island*
- *The north of the island*

ERMOUPOLIS AND ANO SYROS

ERMOUPOLIS: LAYOUT OF THE CITY

Prosperous, business-like, and at the same time urbanely elegant, the port of Syros is quite different in feel and appearance from the other Cycladic towns. There is no enervating preponderance of tourism, no cultivated prettiness, but rather a dignified, busy, working town which still conserves many of the areas of striking beauty conceived by its builders. '*[H]ermou-polis*', the 'city of Hermes'—presiding divinity of commerce and communication—aptly fulfills the name chosen for it by its founders in the 19th century. Ermoúpolis is the administrative capital of the prefecture of the Cyclades Islands, and consequently one of the most important communications centres of the Aegean.

From the arriving boat, the lay-out and genesis of the city can be seen at a glance. In the centre, is the deep curve of the old harbour, protected by a projecting natural mole—the **Nisáki**—to its east. Around the harbour's northern and western sides spread the city of **Ancient Syros** or **Syra**. Far above and behind it to the left-hand side, on top of a natural acropolis crowned by the severe architecture of the church of Aghios Giorgios, is the

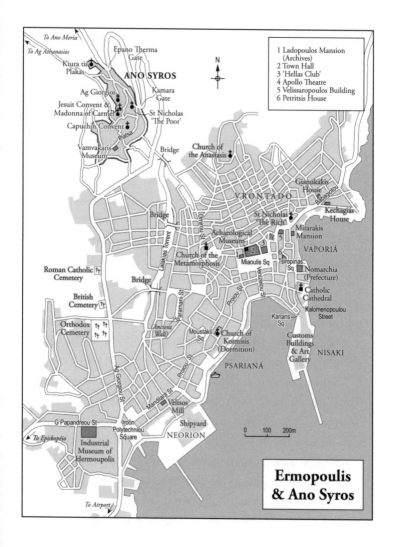

To Ano Meria

To Ag Athanasios

Epano Therma
Gate

Kiura tis
Plakas

ANO SYROS

Ag Giorgios

Kamara
Gate

Jesuit Convent &
Madonna of Carmel

St Nicholas
'The Poor'

Capuchin Convent

Vamvakaris
Museum

Bridge

Church of
the Anastasis

1 Ladopoulos Mansion
  (Archives)
2 Town Hall
3 'Hellas Club'
4 Apollo Theatre
5 Velissaropoulos Building
6 Petritsis House

Gianukakis
House

VRONTADO

Babagiotou

Bridge

St Nicholas
'The Rich'

Kechagias
House

Mitarakis
Mansion

Achaeological
Museum

Roman Catholic
Cemetery

Church of the
Metamorphosis

Miaoulis Sq

VAPORIÁ

Tsiropinas
Sq

Nomarchia
(Prefecture)

British
Cemetery

Bridge

Catholic
Cathedral

Orthodox
Cemetery

Kalomenopoulou
Street

Kanaris
Sq

Moustakli
Sq

Church of
Koimisis
(Dormition)

Customs
Buildings
& Art
Gallery

NISAKI

PSARIANÁ

G Papandreou St

Iroön
Polytechniou
Square

Veltsos
Mill

Shipyard

0   100   200m

To Episkopéio

Industrial
Museum of
Hermoupolis

NEORION

To Airport

Lalakias Torrent

Tommy St

Paramani St

Venizelou St

Proiou St

Ag Giorgiou St

Mandrara St

Proiou St

Ancient
Wall

**Ermopoulis
& Ano Syros**

mediaeval town of **Ano Syros** ('Upper Syros'), much of which was created by Italian settlers in the 13th century; while along the waterfront to the north and south, and up the hill immediately behind, extends the city of **Ermoupolis**, founded in the second decade of the 19th century largely by refugee mariners and ship-owners from the island of Chios: hence the names of the stylish, neoclassical, residential neighbourhoods behind the shore to the north of the Nisaki mole—'**Vapória**' ('steam-ships'), and '**Vrontádo**', named after the shore to the north of the port of Chios, from which so many of the new settlers came. To the south of the town, stretch the commercial areas of Ermoupolis: first, the *Neórion*, or ship-yard, which occupies a projection in the centre of the sweep of the bay; immediately to its north is the densely inhabited area of **Psarianá**, founded and named by the second great influx of refugees, this time from the island of Psará; while to the south of the shipyards lie the decommissioned warehouses, tanneries and factories of the 19th century city's industrial heart. Finally, on a rise in the middle of the south shore of the bay, appropriately detached from the rest of the conurbation, stands the *Lazareto*, or quarantine hospital, built in 1839/40, since then used as a prison and a mad-house, and now in a state of abandon, awaiting transformation into a casino.

THE WATERFRONT & MAIN SQUARE—
PLATEIA MIAOULIS

The modest harmonious assemblage of buildings along the harbour's waterfront—mostly of neoclassical inspiration, with balconies of marble and wrought iron, and occasional, hesitant pediments—dates from the third and fourth decades of the 19th centuries when the irregular shore of the bay was given a more precise, constructed form with promenades and wharfs. The Chiot refugees who constructed much of Ermoupolis naturally wanted to create it in the image of what they had been forced to leave behind. The harbour-front at Chios, today mostly rebuilt with unattractive constructions of the 1960s and 70s, would once have been a grander version of this style of architecture.

From the centre of the northern side of the harbour, the broad, marble-paved **Venizélou Street** cuts perpendicularly in from the waterfront across the principal commercial streets of the market area to the city's heart and architectural show-piece, ***Plateia Miaoúlis**—a grand public space which is somewhat unexpected in the context of a Cycladic island. Similar in aspects to the main-square of Nauplion, this is one of the most elegant and architecturally homogeneous 19th century squares in Greece. In its classicising buildings and ground-floor arcades it imitates the style of a northern Italian city, while the curious marble band-stand, erected at the turn of the 20th century, lends a Central European note. In its material, however—the Cycladic marble of the façades and paving—there is an unmistakably Greek accent. Of an evening the square is animated by the *volta*—the evening constitutional or *passeggiata* of local citizenry, while during the daytime its shady porticos are thronged with café-life. The square first took shape in the 1840s; it was first paved with white and grey marble from Tinos in 1868. Its dedication in 1889 to the Hydriot admiral and independence hero, Andreas Miaoulis, whose suave statue by Giorgios Bonanos is the centrepiece of the square, superseded previous dedications first to King Otho, and subsequently to the anti-monarchical activist Nikolaos Leotsakos, who had sought to remove the king. Ermoupolis was one of the principal poles of opposition to the government of Capodistrias and to the increasingly wayward King Otho.

The last building to be constructed was the massive **Town Hall** on the north side, which today dominates the square and whose rectilinear form is given relief by the palm-trees and the activity of the cafés on its ground-floor. It was built at considerable expense, between 1876 and 1889—a period in which the fortunes of the city were already in decline. Instrumental in its completion was the energetic and autocratic mayor, Dimitrios Vafiadakis, whose name is memorialised in the inscription on the front of the building.

> The design is by the German architect, Ernst Ziller (1837–1923), who was responsible for a great many of the grandly classicising, municipal and royal buildings in Greece, and was Professor of Architecture for over four decades at the Athens *Polytechneion*. Questions of cost meant that Ziller's design was more than once modified from his original plan. His earliest drawings do not include the imposing—almost disproportionately large—staircase on the south façade. The interior, perfectly symmetrical in plan, incorporates pillared courts and patios in Tinos marble. It is of a self-consciously spacious grandeur, expressive of the municipal pride and prosperity of the city in the 19th century. A number of Ziller's drawings for the building are exhibited in the Industrial Museum of Ermoupolis (*see below*).

The Town Hall is flanked by structures less grandiose, but no less interesting architecturally: the **Hellas Club** (now the Municipal Library and Cultural Centre), designed and built by the Italian architect Pietro Sampò in the 1860s, stands to its east side, and was originally conceived as a meeting place for the businessmen of the city on the model of a London Club. In spite of damage from bombardment during the Second World War, the interior—in particular the ballroom on the first floor—still preserves its original pictorial decorations. To the west side of the Town Hall, in similar architectural style, is the **Ladopoulos Mansion** (1870), which now houses the Historical Archives of the Cyclades. A flight of marble steps leads up between these two buildings: at the top on the right is the entrance to the **Archaeological Museum of Syros** which occupies the northwest corner of the Town Hall building (*open daily, except Mon, 8.30–3*). The museum, which was one of the first to be created in the islands, was begun in 1834 around the nucleus of a private collection and was moved to its present location at the beginning of the last century. There are four rooms.

The strength of the museum is its collection of Early Cycladic material, most of which is exhibited in *Room II*, to the right of the entrance. The centre-piece is the sharply defined Early Cycladic II **female figurine** in marble from Naxos, remarkably complete, though with a small break at the neck. From the cemetery of **Chalandrianí** on Syros, there are stone vases, ceramic pots, obsidian blades and dishes of the late 4th and 3rd millennia BC, as well as a considerable number of bronze pins, tweezers, and bronze chisels, produced by the workshops of Early Bronze Age **Kastrí**. An **Egyptian statue** of a priest in black granite dating from the end of the 22nd Dynasty (early 8th century BC) is also exhibited. *Room I* (entrance vestibule) contains Hellenistic and Roman finds and inscriptions from Syros. Of particular interest is the fragment of an **altar to Isis** whose decorative design incorporates sistrum-motifs. In *Room III* (ahead), which contains finds from around the Cyclades, a number of the most interesting pieces are from Amorgos: two fine, 1st century AD, **portrait-heads of Drusus** and of **Agrippina**; a fragmentary marble image of striking clarity of a **man holding a horse by a bridle**; a

Hellenistic **votive relief** showing a sacrifice being made to a mounted hero, whose dramatic pose is reminiscent of the riders in the Parthenon frieze. Also from Amorgos is the fragmentary, early Archaic inscription, engraved from right to left on a limestone block.

The last room features a permanent exhibition of the important work and finds of the pioneering Greek archaeologist, **Christos Tsoundas** (1857–1934) at Chalandrianí and Kastrí on Syros. After distinguished work at Mycenae and Tiryns, Tsoundas turned his attention to burial sites in the Cyclades. His research and finds led him to give a clear and lasting identity to Early Bronze Age culture in the Islands, which he termed

'Cycladic civilisation'. He was responsible for the majority of early archaeological work on Syros. Among the exhibits from his excavations are some very fine examples of the so-called **'frying-pan' pots** with refined surface decorations, dating from the second half of the 3rd millennium BC. The purpose of these unusual objects is still debated, but their curious shape may possibly be a representation of the womb: some examples (not exhibited here) have surface decoration with what appears to some to be the female pubic triangle. There are also marble mortars for the grinding of pigments; and **two-handled chalices** or '*depas*' cups, contemporaneous with and similar in design to those found at Poliochni on Lemnos, and in the Troad.

FROM NISAKI, THROUGH VAPORIA, TO PLATEIA MIAOULIS

The marble-paved streets and balconied houses of Ermoupolis are a pleasure to explore. A sense of their variety can be appreciated in the walk traced below which begins by the breakwater in the southeast corner of the harbour.

'Nisáki', the rocky finger of land which defines the eastern border of the harbour, was originally detached from the town as its name meaning 'islet' implies. In the late

1830s it was levelled, widened and joined to the rest of the harbour, so as to accommodate the new **Customs Buildings** and **storehouses** of the port. These sober buildings combine unobtrusive dignity with functionality: one of them now houses the **Art Gallery of the Cyclades** (*open 10–1, 7–10: entrance (free) on the east side*) dedicated to the exhibition of works by local artists. A visit affords the possibility of seeing the magnificent brick-vaulted spaces of the interior, and the multicolour patchwork of local stone used in constructing the walls. From the seaward side of Nisáki, the stone **lighthouse** (29.5m in height) of the islet of Gaidouronisi (also called Didymi), built in 1834, can be seen a short distance out to sea. Beyond are the silhouettes of Tinos, Rhenia and Mykonos. Nisaki also affords a good view of the sweep of fine houses along the front of Vaporia to its north and east. The main street which leads from Nisáki towards Vaporia, **Kalomenopoúlou Street**, contains a number of notable buildings, beginning with the **Catholic Cathedral** of the Annunciation (1829) on the corner of Evangelistrias Street, with its façade surmounted by a silhouette of scrolls and volutes. Just to its north are the buildings of the **National Bank** (1907), and of the **Catholic Hospice** (1904), which replaced, on the same site, the earliest seat of the Municipality before it was moved to the main square. Ka-

lomenopoulou Street ends in a small square, which takes
its name, **Plateia Tsiropinás**, from the fine **neoclassical
building** on its east side, now occupied by the *Nomarchia or Prefecture of the Cyclades, built as a residence
in 1883/4 for the Tsiropinas and Salustros families. The
low beautifully proportioned façade is articulated with a
central monumental doorway in Ionic style, and with an
ornamental attic balustrade surmounted with 'Palladian'
statues. Another of the city's most striking private houses
stands 30m beyond the west end of Tsiropinás Square
on the north side of Souri Street which leads back to the
main square: this is the two storey marble **residence of the
Petritzis family** (1878), constructed in grey marble with
chamfered corners. The arcaded lower floor, designed for
commercial use, is surmounted by an upper residential
storey with refined rectangular window-frames in marble
as well as a decorative parapet to complete the design. A
similarity of idiom between the lower floor of this building and the arcaded warehouses opposite it, shows that
both were designed by the same architect, Konstantinos
Kokkinis. The upper floor of the residence was added a
decade later by a different architect, Dimitrios Elefth-
eriadis.

We continue north along Apollonos Street from the
Nomarchia building, passing the elegant **Giasemoladás**

Mansion, with its restored decorative refinements and deeply inset entrance, protected by an iron and glass roof. On the right side, shortly before the street emerges into the square in front of the church at its north end, is the **Mitarakis Mansion**: its early date (c. 1827) means that its style is more Levantine than neoclassical, with an upper floor in wood and plaster, and large wood-framed windows with lunettes which enclose what was originally an open verandah.

The area of Vapória is dominated by the grandiose church of **Aghios Nikólaos o Ploúsios** (St Nicholas 'the Rich' or 'Magnificent', so as to differentiate it from the older church of Aghios Nikólaos o Ptochós, St Nicholas 'the Poor' in Ano Syros). It was designed by Gerasimos Metaxas in 1848, constructed and decorated over the subsequent 60 years, and underwritten by contributions from King Otho of Greece, the Greek community in Russia, the citizens of Chios and other benefactors.

The façade and portico, constructed in Pentelic and Tinos marble, are in rigorously classicising style; the idiom is preserved in the pilasters, capitals and window-frames on the sides of the building, giving the church impressive architectural unity. The church is a domed, three-aisle basilica, with a highly decorated interior, dominated by a grand iconostasis in Pentelic marble (1871), which is partially gilded and embellished with a variety of polychrome marbles. The painted icons by different artists of the mid-19th century are fine examples of their kind, and the suitably rich icon of the patron saint is of a scale to match the aspirations and title of the church.

East of the church of St Nicholas, **Babagiotou Street** opens onto the rise above the waterfront and is lined on its landward side by fine, two- and three-storey, neo-classical houses of grand proportions, conserving their wrought-iron work and the painted ceilings of their interiors, a number of which now serve as stylish hotels.

In front of the west entrance of St Nicholas the Rich, a small park of palm-trees and pines surrounds a **monument to the Unburied Warrior** of the Greek revolution: this is a work by the sculptor Giorgios Vitalis in 1858, based on the model of the typical Hellenistic tomb surmounted by a recumbent lion. From here, the southwestern exit of the square (Aghios Nikolaos Street) leads down towards Plateia Miaoulis once again. On the left side after 30m is the three-storey marble façade of the **Velissaropoulos Building** (1871). As in the Patritzis Building, the ground floor which was dedicated to trade has tall, arched openings forming a frontal arcade; the residential floors above have much decorative detail, including coffering on the underside of the marble balconies; and the interior has fine decorative paintings. Just beyond, the street opens into an area occupied by the **Apollo Theatre**—an unostentatious building created by the Italian architect Pietro Sampò in 1862, who clearly had in mind, particularly as regards the interior of the building, the designs of some of the great Italian theatres such as the Teatro San Carlo in Naples. The building was a symbol of the cultural 'coming of age' of the town of Ermoupolis. Its structure was damaged during the war, then badly restored, and is now undergoing a second more sensitive and historically accurate restoration in the interior. From in front of the theatre, Melina Merkouri Street leads down into the east side of Plateia Miaoulis once again.

THE CHURCH OF THE METAMORPHOSIS &
PSARIANA

From slightly above the northwest corner of Plateia Miaoúlis, Politis Street leads west to the **cathedral of the Metamorphosis of the Saviour** (Transfiguration). A number of the windows in this and adjacent streets have ballooning, scroll-shaped, protective cages in wrought-iron which permit those inside to lean out and participate in street life. Like the church of St Nicholas the Rich, the Metamorphosis is also raised on a high platform, built out from the steep slope of the hill. It was the first large church to be built in the city.

The church, which still functions as the island's Orthodox cathedral, was begun in 1824 and completed by 1831. The new city was officially baptised 'Ermoupolis' in 1826 at a ceremony in the large forecourt to the east of the church, which is attractively cobbled with black and white pebbles brought from Rhodes. The largest bell in the church's two towers which preside over the neighbourhood of Psarianá to the west, appropriately comes from the original church of St Nicholas on Psará which was destroyed in the Turkish attack of 1824. The interior, entered through a vestibule on the south side, is in three aisles separated by monolithic marble columns: the first two columns (behind the iconostasis) are ancient and come from Delos. The baptismal font is also an adapted ancient plinth which once supported a bust of Hadrian: the bust itself was carried away from the island by Russian officers during the Russo Turkish war of 1768–74. The marble iconostasis and the icons themselves—though none predates the mid 19th century—are of high quality.

If the cathedral of the Metamorphosis functions as the

ceremonial church of the city, the lighter and more elegant church of the **Koimisis tis Theotokou** (Dormition) is Psarianá's 'neighbourhood church'. It stands on
the north side of Proiou Street (one full block inland
from the harbour-front at the level of the main bus sta-
tion, near the ferry embarkations). The church was begun
in 1828, only four years after the cathedral; its shell is in
marble, while the roof and interior columns are in wood.
The arcades along its west and south sides, originally
open, have now been closed with wrought-iron gates.
The church's treasure is the *patronal icon** from which
the church takes its name: it is displayed beside the doorway in the atrium, and is an image of the Dormition of
the Virgin, painted by the barely 20 year-old Domenikos
Theotokopoulos, later known in the west as El Greco. The
icon would be of note for its artistic qualities even if its
authorship were not known: the stylisation of figure and
pose and grouping is beautifully orchestrated, creating a
moving tension to the design. The drapery is gracefully
conceived. There is a striking similarity between the general lay-out of the subject matter of the icon, and that
in El Greco's most famous painting, the *Burial of Count
Orgaz* (1586), in Toledo: the comparison underlines how
dramatically far the artist's style and imaginative world
developed. A lack of unified perspective is characteristic

of icon-painting: later in his career, El Greco was also to eliminate any suggestion of geometric perspective from his paintings. The signature is around the base of the candelabrum. The icon dates from c. 1562 and was probably brought to Syros from Psará by refugees.

The church of the Koimisis—according to a topography of the ancient city suggested by the 19th century scholar, Klon Stephanos—stands over the site of the *agora* and *prytaneion* of Ancient *Syros*. Seats from the ancient theatre have also been found and conserved in the basement of the building on the corner of Kleisthénous and Kosmás Streets; a small section of the **ancient fortification wall** is also visible in the base of the wall at the southeast corner of the Stadium of the High School on Paramani Street. The continuation of Proiou Street approximately three blocks to the southwest of the church of the Koimisis passes through the line of the ancient walls at what would have been the ancient city's southern gateway.

Today Proiou Street ends further south, almost at the shipyards: it continues as **Mandilará Street** which leads into the industrial area of the 19th century city. Almost immediately to the left off Mandilará, is the entrance to the *Neorion*, or shipyard, established almost 150 years ago in 1861. The spacious original block, designed by Pietro Sampò, comprising the iron foundry still forms the core of the complex, though it has been expanded considerably since then. The addition of a floating iron shipyard in 1953 notably increased the capacity of the yards. Used today for re-fitting and repairs rather than construction, the yards are still active and constitute a major player in the island's economy. Immediately beyond the entrance to the *Neorion* on Mandilara Street is one of the many warehouses which once populated the area: the front of the (disused) **Veltsos Flour Mill**—an elegantly pedimented, square façade of three floors with large, arched windows framed in brick—is expressive of the dignified optimism characteristic of the early industrial period in Europe. The unselfconscious inclusion of artistic elements in functional buildings is typified by the unexpectedly beautiful **marble relief** and medallion above the door, by the sculptor Giorgios Vitalis. The Mill was built in 1865 and functioned up until 1899.

Mandilará Street and its continuation south along **Iróön Polytechníou Street** (the main road out to the airport and to Mána) pass by the remains of many of the factories, warehouses and industrial sites which brought settlers, wealth and employment to the island in the 19th century—textile factories, tanneries, silk-works, and establishments for the production of gunpowder, gunshot or for the processing of emery from Naxos. All are now in disuse. The diversity and energy of this industrial culture is memorialised in the newly opened **Industrial Museum of Hermoupolis** at 11 G. Papandreou Street, just west of Iroön Square at the end of Mandilará Street. (*Open daily, 10–2, and 6–9 Thurs and Sun, closed Tues. Reduced hours in winter.*) The museum's well laid-out and labelled displays occupy five rooms on the ground floor of the former Katsimandís paint and colour factory, and pay tribute to the remarkable commercial dynamism of Syros in the four decades between 1860 and 1900. (Notice, on entering the building, the middle doorstep whose upper surface is carved with the **graffito** of a ship and the legend '*E. BENHZE/ΛΟΣ*' (sic). The family of Eleftherios Venizelos, Greece's elder statesman and prime minister during the first three decades of the last century, fled to Syros from Crete in 1866 and the young Eleftherios was a student at the *Gymnasion* of Ermoupolis in 1879/80. The alternative spelling of the name in the graffito with an '*H*', rather than an '*I*', however, suggests that the man himself may not necessarily have been its author.)

The museum displays **architects' drawings and water-colours** for the important public buildings of the city—the theatre, the meat-markets, the shipyards etc. Amongst them are Ernst Ziller's designs for the Town Hall. The examples of **industrial machinery**—printing-presses, engines, looms, machines for patisserie and for embroidery—are objects often of beauty. A number were made in England, underscoring Syros's historic links with London and Manchester, in the fields of technology, banking and insurance. The **photographs** exhibited show the port in its heyday, with over two dozen cargo steamships moored side by side (1931), and with the newly commissioned floating-dock (1953).

THE CEMETERIES

Less than a kilometre from Plateia Iroön, to the west side of the main road (Od. Aghiou Giorgiou) which leads to the north of the island, are the city's three cemeteries—Orthodox, Catholic and British—which are of interest both for their history and monumental sculpture. The **Orthodox Cemetery** (the first and largest of the three) which lies to the south side of the church of Aghios Giorgios (1839), constitutes one of the most evocative assemblages of **funerary sculpture** in Greece, comparable in the Islands perhaps only to the cemetery of Andros (*see p. 25*). Contemporary with the other great 'artistic' provincial cemeteries of Europe—such as Glasgow's Western Necropolis and the cemetery of Staglieno in Genoa—the flowering of grand, classicising tombs here was a product of the prosperity and cosmopolitan connections of Syros in the last four decades of the 19th century. It involved the participation of a number of the period's most important sculptors, in particular Giorgios Vitalis from Tinos (1841–1900), who was responsible for the monuments of the Vafiadakis, Avgherinos, Ladopoulos, Arangkis, Tsiropinas and Chrisos families. Some of the monuments are in the form of small Classical temples; others are refined sarcophagi with recumbent or lamenting figures of angels. The beauty of these objects lies in a simple counterpoint of precise geometric shapes juxtaposed with the irregular forms of flowing drapery, sculpted urns, or human figures. The peaceful melancholy of the sculptures and the contrast of the white marble with the dark cypress trees and palms create an atmosphere of rare elegiac beauty.

A short distance beyond to the north is the inconspicuous entrance to the **British Cemetery**. At the front are the simple burials of a number of early British residents who were drawn to the island by the strong links in maritime business between Syros and the commercial centres of Britain. In a separate area behind are the graves of sailors and soldiers who died in military action in the Aegean in the three years following the Gallipoli campaign of

1915—many of whom died at sea when the transporter, SS. *Arcadian*, on its way from Thessalonica to Alexandria was torpedoed by a German submarine and sank in April 1917. A little further north again along the street is the **Catholic Cemetery**, also with a number of interesting sculptural monuments marking the burials of French, Italian and Greek Catholic families.

ANO SYROS

(Ano Syros—Upper or Old Syros—lies to the northwest of Ermoupolis and is a 30–40 minute, uphill walk from the harbour-front. From the western side of the church of the Metamorphosis (west of Plateia Miaoúlis), follow **Odós Omirou** *all the way north out of Ermoupolis, across the La-lakiás valley—noting the fine 19th century marble bridges which cross the torrent-bed—and continue up the steps into the eastern side of Ano Syros. The alternative is to go by car or taxi as far as the highest point of Ano Syros and to enter by the 'Epano Terma' entrance. For the sake of simplicity the itinerary below assumes entry at this point, i.e. at the top of the village.)*

Ano Syros has today the typical form and appearance of a mediaeval Cycladic '*kastro*', even though the hill which it occupies was probably inhabited as a refuge from sea-borne Saracen raids, as early as the 8th or 9th century. Its present semi-fortified appearance with gateways was given it by the 13th century Italian settlers on the island following the establishment of Marco Sanudo's Duchy of Naxos to which the island belonged. The community's original religious culture was Roman Catholic and remains predominantly so today, in contrast to Orthodox Ermoupolis. The town must have expanded down the hill from the summit, hence its roughly concentric plan of streets on successive levels. The houses are constructed mostly on two floors accommodated against the steep slope: the living and sleeping rooms are generally on the upper floor, and the utilitarian or commercial spaces on the ground floor. The streets are narrow and often stepped, and pass frequently beneath covered passages called '*ste[g]ádia*': the open spaces are few and intimate. The settlement and its lay-out, with a deep gorge to the east side where the principal spring rises, has similarities to the Chora of Seriphos. But Ano Syros lacks the customary vitality of an island chora, because its role has been usurped by Ermoupolis. Several paths lead down both from the top of the town and from the Portara Gate to the **springs** below the church of **Aghios Athanasios** deep in the cleft on the east side. The water is soft and very slightly brackish: it gives rise to clusters of citrus trees, plane trees and vigorous caper bushes in the protected declivity.

At the northernmost extremity of Ano Syros, just outside the **Epano Terma** entrance is the small 17th century chapel of **Kiurá tis Plákas**, belonging to the Jesuit Order: on a panoramic terrace to its north is a bust honouring Pherecydes of Syros (fl. c. 550 BC), the mythographer and thinker who may have been the mentor of Pythagoras. Turning south into Ano Syros, the narrow street leads directly to the summit dominated by the church of **Aghios Giorgios** from whose terrace a magnificent view over the bay of Ermoupolis and the neighbouring islands opens out. The church's massive, fortress-like east wall is visible from far below in Ermoupolis. The building, whose present form dates from a complete rebuilding begun in 1832, replaces an earlier 17th century church on the site, built after the original church was destroyed during Turkish reprisals in 1617. The site has probably been occupied by a church, as well as a fortified watch-tower, since the 13th century. The monolithic marble columns in the west portico are possibly ancient pieces taken from Delos.

The path which descends to the south from Aghios Giorgios circumvents the large block of the **Jesuit Convent** which was founded in 1744, and passes in front of the neoclassical façade of the church of the **Madonna of**

Mount Carmel: the whole of the marble façade, with the exception of the 17th century door-frame, was re-made in 1824 by the same architect who designed the front of the Evangelistria Catholic Church in Vaporia in a somewhat similar style. The marble **window-lights** carved as sunbursts are an unusual, virtuoso feature. Descending further, past the churches of St Anthony and of **St Nicholas 'the Poor'**—both 18th century buildings recently restructured—you come to the attractive, roofed passage of the **Kamara Gate**. From here the ambiguously named '*Piatsa*'—which is more the main street of Ano Syros than a closed square—runs south and west to the Portara Gate in the west, passing in front of the community's Town Hall about half-way between the two. To the left at a junction just beyond the Town Hall is the small **museum** dedicated to **Markos Vamvakaris**, one of the pioneering masters of *rebétiko* music, and of the *bouzouki*. (*Open daily, June–end Sept 10–2.30, 7–11.30.*) The museum is a collection of photographs and personalia which reflect the simplicity of the musician's origins and his dedication to the music he helped to make famous.

MARKOS VAMVAKARIS

Vamvakaris—known to aficionados of *rebetika*, just
as 'Markos'—was born into a humble Catholic family of Ano Syros in 1905. At the age of 13 he left Syros
as a stowaway on a boat for Piraeus, where he found
occasional work first as a stevedore in the port and
then as a labourer in a slaughterhouse. He taught
himself to play the *bouzouki* (a type of large oriental
mandolin with a shimmering richness of tone) and
by the late 1920s was performing in night locales and
hashish dens in Piraeus. Here he came into contact
with refugees from Greek Asia Minor. He rapidly absorbed their compelling and nostalgic lyrics, which
were born, like the Delta 'Blues', from a keen sense
of dispossession, and began in 1932 making the first
recordings of *rebetiko* and *bouzouki* music, as well as
composing his famous love-songs known as '*Frango-
syriani*' in which he recalls the island of his birth. The
name refers to the Catholic inhabitants ('*Frango-*', literally 'Frankish') of Syros ('*-syriani*').

With their frequent references to the drink, drugs
and crime of the urban subculture, *rebetika* have
inevitably attracted the attention of censors during

the periods of restrictive politics and military rule in Greece; but they have recently enjoyed a deserved renaissance in the last three decades. *Rebetiko* is a compression of many of the deep sentiments evoked by the country's recent history, and is one of the most redolent sounds of night-spots in Greece. Vamvakaris's distinctive, rough voice and brilliant mastery of the *bouzouki* make him one of the greatest interpreters of the spirit of *rebetiko*. He died in 1972; the museum was established in 1995.

THE SOUTH OF THE ISLAND

(*Plateia Iroön, Ermoupolis = 0.0km for distances in text*)

The southern portion of the island, in vivid contrast to the steep, wild north, is a gentler landscape of hills and valleys, cultivated and inhabited wherever possible. It has a prevailingly recreational character imparted by the scattered 19th century villas and the pleasant coastal resorts around its perimeter.

The road which heads due west from the main roundabout of Plateia Iroön by the shipyards of Ermoupolis, climbs swiftly into the interior to a junction (2.3km) marked to the left for **Episkopeío** (3km), which takes its name from a former country-residence of the bishop of Syros. One of the island's strongest springs rises here and has created a valley full of gardens and stone villas, shaded with mature trees, some of which are in a state of romantic abandon. To the right of the road amongst pines, stands the **Kouloukoundis Mansion** with an arcaded verandah on two floors, shaded by wooden eaves and decorations of Balkan Ottoman style. Beyond it are other, stone-built villas, all with a dignified symmetry of design and lush vegetation fed by the copious spring. At the head of the valley is the 19th century church of Prophitis Elias and, to the south side, the attractive 17th century **church of the Assumption**.

Shortly after returning to the main road and continuing to climb, the road for **Alithiní** (4km) branches to the right, affording a panoramic **view** of almost the whole of Ermoupolis below. Tinos, Mykonos, Rheneia, Naxos and Paros are all visible on the horizon in good weather conditions: the view is particularly striking at night. Alithiní is one of the two spots on the island where Pherecydes is believed to have lived a hermitic existence in a cave (*see below, pp. 144–145*). Ancient architectural elements found in the area of the village have led scholars to suggest that the sanctuary to the Cabiri, alluded to frequently in the image repertoire of Hellenistic coinage from Syros, may have been here.

After the turning for Alithini the road crosses the watershed of the island and passes a large open **quarry** which, together with those of Tinos, has provided most of the material for the buildings and paving of Ermoupolis. The road drops swiftly to the protected bay and resort of **Kíni** (7km) which faces attractively towards the setting sun. Boats from here can be arranged for visiting the more inaccessible coves, beaches, and points of interest (such as Grámmata—*see pp. 149–151*) in the north of the island. From above Kíni the road continues south to **Galissás** (10.5km) which lies at the head of a long deep inlet. On the westernmost rise of the promontory of Cape Kataképhalos to the north side of the bay, stand the ruins of a **mediaeval fortress** which served as watchtower for the western coast of the island. The most ancient presence in the area, however, has been identified near the small headland of Aghia Pakoú immediately to the south of the bay where there are two natural acropolises—the projecting hilltop crowned by the church of Aghia Pakoú, and the higher rise of 'Vounáki' behind and to the south.

Archaeological examination has shown that this was the site
of a densely inhabited ancient settlement in the Archaic and
Classical periods, which some scholars think should possibly
be identified as the ancient polis of *Syros*. The centre of habitation from the 8th century BC on was on the saddle below
Vounaki and on the hilltop now occupied by the church of
Aghia Pakou. The hill is perforated with shallow grottos. The
ancient buildings so far excavated (beside the path which
descends to the bay of Armeos on the west side) were partly
cut into the living rock, to create cisterns etc., and partly
constructed. The dedication, '*Aghia Pakou*', is unusual; it
may possibly be cognate with the ancient word '*ἐπιχωρέω*',
('I assent' or 'concede'), in view of the fact that epigraphic
evidence suggests that a divinity with the attribute '*ἐ[πιχώ]
ος*' ('assenting') is attested here. The remains of a small **Early
Cycladic II** settlement on the summit of Vounaki is evidence
of even earlier occupation.

From the waterfront at Galissás it is possible to take a
boat to visit the attractive cave-church of **Aghios Stéph-
anos**, 1km along the coast to the west. The chapel is built
under the lea of an overhanging rock beside the entrance
to a natural grotto a few metres above the water-level.

South of Galissás, the landscape changes rapidly be-
coming lower and more fertile as the road drops down

to **Fínikas** (13.5km) which is set in a wider and shallower bay, dotted with outlying islands. The particularly sheltered position of the harbour was appreciated in Antiquity, something which has been confirmed by recent underwater archaeological exploration which has revealed not only deposits of Classical, Hellenistic and Byzantine amphorae but also the remains of an ancient harbour mole 65m long and c. 2.50m wide. Early Cycladic settlement is also attested on the offshore island of Schinónisi.

The tranquillity of both sea and landscape in this area attracted an intense colonisation of the southern side of the bay during the 19th century. The wealthy families of Ermoupolis created the summer resort here of '**Delagratsia**' ('Della Grazia'), now renamed—a little unimaginatively—**Poseidonía** (15km). At the height of its fashion (1880), there was even talk of linking the resort to Ermoupolis with a steam railway. The result was the planting of numerous **country villas** in the area, often designed in the highly eclectic architecture of the period which has close parallels with that of the large Athenian suburban villas in Kifissia. Castellated towers, large verandahs, steeply projecting eaves, and rooms with high windows and ceilings are the staple architectural vocabulary of these buildings. It is a curious architecture whose origins are various: part a reaction to, and liberation from,

the sober symmetry of the neoclassical urban architecture (hence the prevailing asymmetry); part a whimsical
bourgeois desire to possess 'a castle' (towers and crenel-
lations); and part an emulation of the atmosphere of
Middle-European and Balkan resorts (conical roofs and
pronounced eaves). Of particular note are the '**Poseidonia Club**' (1913); the **Tsiropinas Villa** set amid a park of
pine-trees and palms; the **Muncipality** (ex-Villa Dask-
ou); the **Valmas Villa** with its conspicuous red tower; the
more neoclassical **Aranghis Villa**; and the grandiloquent
turreted **Ladopoulos** and **Giorgiadis Villas**. More villas,
predominantly neoclassical in style, some landscaped
and terraced in mature parks, are to be found scattered
through the villages of the interior: at **Parakopí** (Vessaro-
poulos Villa); at **Chroúsa** (Vafiadakis and Papadakis Villas); and at **Vári** and **Ano Mána**: their exploration constitutes one of the pleasures of a visit to Syros.

By the direct, cross-country route via Messariá, Poseidonia is only 10km from Ermoupolis: otherwise it is
14km by the continuation of the main road via the island's south coast which passes through the resorts of
Mégas Gialós and **Vári** and returns to Ermoupolis, passing the airport and finally the melancholy succession of
ruined, 19th century warehouses and factories along the
southwest shore of the port.

THE NORTH OF THE ISLAND

The unexpectedly steep and mountainous north of the island is a sparsely inhabited, Cycladic landscape of steep valleys, exiguous villages and superb views. In theory the area can be explored though a network of footpaths; but these are mostly not signed and can be ill-defined in places. Patience and perseverance is needed. Most of the important sites are best accessible by a combination of car and walking. The (only) road to the north leaves from Plateia Iroön, climbs steeply past Ano Syros (2km) and on up the deep cleft in the island to the north of the capital, as far as the watershed at **Mýtakas** (4.5km) which lies just below the island's highest summit of Mount Pyrgos (442 m) to its southwest. (The branch road west through Mytakas leads steeply down the western slope of the island to the remote and panoramic cluster of houses at **Hartianá** (6.5km), from where a path leads down to the delightful beach of **Delfíni**.) Seven hundred metres beyond Mytakas a track leads right to the village of **Rychopós** which overlooks the east coast. From the village a clear footpath leads north in 15 minutes to the '**cave of Pherecydes**'. (*The unsigned cave can easily be missed, because it is hidden from view. After the path ceases descending and levels*

out, there is a wall of rock to the left side of the path: a steep
scramble over the rocks here up to a ledge visible above the
path, leads to where the cave is.) The cave is low and shallow: it is said the philosopher practiced an ascetic existence here. Another cave at Alithiní is also said perhaps to
have been his dwelling.

THE CAVES OF PHERECYDES

Pherecydes of Syros appears to have flourished in the
mid 6th century BC, if not earlier. He belongs to a
period in which Greek thinking was only beginning
to distinguish between poetic mythology and what it
later called philosophy: in fact, Aristotle in his *Meta-
physics* characterises the work of Pherecydes as a
mixture of the two. Pherecydes was interested in the
origins of the cosmos, and explained this in allegori-
cal fashion in his principal work, the *Pentemychos* or
Heptamychos (the 'Five' or 'Seven Recesses') which is
only known to us through fragmentary citations or
references in other writers. It was considered to be
one of the first works of Greek prose. It has points
of comparison with Hesiod's *Theogeny*, but appears
to have had a more logical scheme to it. Pherecydes's
interest in the immortality and transmigration of

the human soul, alluded to by Cicero and Augustine, has led to his close association with Pythagoras: Diogenes Laertius says that some considered him to have been the teacher of Pythagoras. Pherecydes is also attributed with having made a *heliotropion*, or sunclock, and is sometimes included as one of the 'Seven Wise Men' of Greece.

A strong tradition in early thinking saw caves, symbolic of darkness and ignorance, as places where illumination could be received. This explains the association of natural grottos such as this (and of another similar cliff-side cave on Samos associated with Pythagoras) with thinkers and philosophers. The tradition remained alive through Christian and Byzantine times in the practices of the Desert Fathers, and in such instances as the Divine Revelation of St John received in a cave on Patmos.

The footpath past the cave continues to the village of **Platy Vouní** (20 mins), one of the most traditional villages of northern Syros, and one of the few that is inhabited all through the year. The village's narrow, walled streets centre on the minuscule church of **Aghios Ioannis Evangelistos**. The church and a number of the older houses and buildings all have roofs in schist blocks. The village is set in a landscape which can have changed little in appearance over the centuries—a configuration of cultivated, walled fields of different colours, textures and shapes, which circle around the flat-topped hill (the '*platys vouno*') to the east. The plateau on the summit was the site of an Early Cycladic settlement.

Platy Vouní can also be reached by car from the right branch off the main road north at Papouri (6km), 1.5km after Mytakas. This road leads (*left*) to the **springs** at Lygeró (7km), and (*right*) to the **Chalandrianí plateau** (7.5km), en route to Platy Vouni (8.5km) where the road ends.

Chalandriani, panoramic and strategically sited overlooking the waters of Andros, Tinos and Mykonos/Delos, was one of the first and most important Early Bronze Age Cycladic sites to be explored in the Islands: it was brought to the attention of the archaeological world after the excavations of the pioneering Greek archaeologist, Christos Tsoundas, in the last decade of the 19th century. Tsoundas uncovered **extensive cemeteries** and artefacts of considerable artistry dating from the Early Cycladic II period (2700–2300 BC). Amongst these were the unusual, so-called **'frying-pan' clay-vessels**, and a number of striking, painted **zoomorphic (?ceremo-**

nial) cups and bowls (now mostly in the National Archeological Museum in Athens). The graves he found were dug into the ground and corbelled—a design unique to Syros.

Little can now be seen of the Bronze Age cemeteries and of the settlement of Chalandriani which lie near to the church of the Panaghia: but on the summit of the precipitous hill to the north, at *****Kastrí**, is one of the most remarkable, fortified, Early Cycladic settlements so far uncovered (*for access, see below*). In 1898 Tsoundas brought to light in this remote site a settlement with an impressive degree of or-

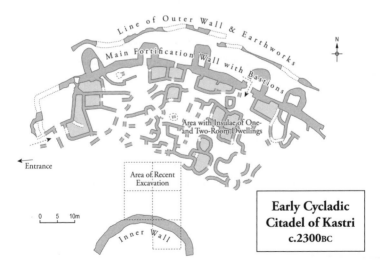

Line of Outer Wall & Earthworks

Main Fortification Wall with Bastions

N

Area with Insulae of One-
and Two-Room Dwellings

← Entrance

Area of Recent
Excavation

0   5   10m

Inner Wall

**Early Cycladic
Citadel of Kastri
c.2300BC**

ganisation and imposing **stone fortifications**. It was smaller and slightly later in date (c. 2300–2200 BC) than the settlement of Chalandriani. The northern edge of the hill is defended with an outwork and semi-circular wall (c. 55m long and 2m high) with six **horseshoe bastions** whose design appears to reflect influence from the Asia Minor coast. Within the walls to the south, the stone, **one or two-room dwellings** are grouped in blocks, and separated by recognisable **streets**. Some of the houses have stone hearths. Significantly, the finding of crucibles for smelting and moulds for casting, as well as many objects in bronze, points to the existence of a flourishing **metalworking shop**. Excavation is still continuing and has brought to light cups, storage vessels, decorated *pyxides*, quern-stones and obsidian blades. The site is dramatic, panoramic, but arduous of access: it inspires admiration for the archaeologists who have worked here.

Access to Kastri (1 hr, by foot from the asphalt road) is only from Chalandriani, and is by a steep and shadeless footpath which descends to sea-level, crosses the torrent-bed, and climbs again to the acropolis across an unstable scree. The site is just below the summit, enclosed by a ring of recent dry-stone walls.

Eight hundred metres north of the turning to Chalandriani off the main road, a left-hand branch leads below a
wind-farm to the village of **Syringas** (8.5km). Of all the
villages of northern Syros, this has the finest panorama:
beyond Gyaros, Kythnos, Kea and Andros, Attica is visible
in the distance. The village is endowed with a spring of
fresh water which gives rise to a small break of vegetation
and reeds; its name is perhaps taken from the nymph, Syr-
inx who, escaping from the attentions of Pan, was turned
into a reed-bed, from which the god subsequently made
his pipe. In local legend the spring is said to be connected
underground with the Sariza source on Andros; its water
is certainly of almost comparable quality.

This northern extremity of the island is also known as
Epáno or Apáno Meriá, the 'Uplands', and comprises a
number of panoramic settlements sown high in the hills
above the sea. The most northerly of them is **Sa** (or San)
Michális (8km) which takes its name from the church of
Aghios Michaïl built beside a curious outcrop of rocks.
Some distance below the road ends at a final cluster of
dwellings at **Kambos** (9km).

From Kambos it is a one hour walk down to what is
one of the most evocative curiosities in the Cyclades—the
site of *Grámmata* (literally meaning 'letters'), a remote
spit of rock whose surface was covered, both in Antiq-

uity and later, by generations of sailors' graffiti and divine invocations. The site is described interestingly in his account of the Cyclades by James Theodore Bent who visited the spot in the autumn of 1882. (*The path is clear at first down to the shore, but subsequently becomes hard to trace as it follows the shoreline, about 10–15m above the water level, round two headlands, as far as the last, westernmost bay which has a small sandy beach. On the promontory of rock which closes the bay to the west side, three smooth, natural 'ramps' are visible. The inscriptions cover these flat surfaces. The site can also be reached in summer by excursion boat from Kini.*) The ***inscriptions** are very many: some modern, some 19th century; but the majority are ancient, written in simple and sensuously rounded lettering. Some are interjections of salvation from sailors who have sought refuge; some are offerings of thanks; some are one-word votives; while others record details of departures or journeys. A number of the later Hellenistic inscriptions are meticulously enclosed by a rectangular frame with two lateral 'wings'. Some have rudimentary drawings of boats, Poseidon's trident, even what appears to be a seven-branch candle-stick. The headland was a crucial landfall for mariners coming from the mainland and its unusually sheltered bay must have been a welcome refuge from an Aegean storm. A small shrine to Asklepi-

os, who is cited in several invocations, may have marked
the promontory. Asklepios is sometimes said to have ac-
companied the Argonauts and was consequently seen as a
protector of mariners—among his many other attributes
of assistance to mankind. The inscriptions may relate to
his cult. The site is curiously compelling; and few other
places can offer such unusual antiquities in addition to
the possibility of a tranquil bathe at the end of an arduous walk.

PRACTICAL INFORMATION

84 100 **Syros**: area 84 sq.km; perimeter 84km; resident population 19,793; max. altitude 442 m. **Port Authorities**: T. 22810 82690. **Travel and information**: Parissis Shipping Agency, T. 22810 82232, 88922

ACCESS

By air: Olympic Air operates 5 weekly flights with small aircraft to Syros; the frequency drops to 3 per week in winter. The airport is 3km from the town.

By boat: As administrative capital of the Cyclades, Syros is well served by sea connections: at least two daily connections by car-ferry (4hrs) or catamaran (2hrs) with Piraeus, and three weekly connections to Rafina. Syros also lies on the ferry routes to: Chios and Lesbos (four times weekly); Tinos and Mykonos (daily); Naxos and Paros (1–2 times daily); and Rhodes (2–4 times weekly). There are also local ferries 3 times weekly which join Syros with the Western Cyclades (Kythnos, Serifos, Siphnos and Milos).

LODGING

Ermoúpolis has several stylish hotels in converted neoclassical mansions in the Vapória district. Three of them are along Babagiótou Street, overlooking the waterfront. The **Syrou Melathron Hotel** (*T. 22810 85963, fax 87806, www.syroumelathron.gr*) at 5 Babagiotou has some grand public rooms and a number of the bedrooms have painted ceilings. More thoughtfully restored is the *****Archontiko Vourli** (*T. 22810 81682, fax 88440*) at 5 Mavrogordá-tou Street (the extension of Babagiotou) which feels more like a house and has beautifully furnished rooms and good breakfasts. These are both relatively expensive options: much simpler and less expensive is the delight-ful **Guesthouse Ypatia** (*T./ fax. 22810 83575*, ipatiaguest@ yahoo.com) at 3 Babagiotou Street. For a simple beach-side hotel outside the city, the **Hotel Poseidonion** (*T. 22810 42100, fax 42220*) at Posei-donía is an unpretentious solution, with pleasant rooms in the new extension behind the hotel. For those in search of unusual and panoramic lodgings, the converted wind-mill, *Anemomylos* (with a/c & kitchen) high up above Ano Syros, can be rented (*T. 22810 80083 or 694 451 5366*).

EATING

The taverna * **San Michalis** in Epáno Meriá deserves recom-mendation both for its mar-vellous sunset views over the tip of Syros and neighbouring islands, and its welcoming service of simple dishes made from local produce. It also serves a very good, local wine (quite strong). Also outside the town, but with a magnificent panorama over it, is **Mitsos** in Alithiní (north off the road to Kíni): its fresh, traditional food is particularly popular with locals, especially at weekends. In Ermoupolis itself, the taverna '**Stin Itháki tou Aï**', hidden in a side-street just east of the main square (Plateia Miaoulis) has imaginative local dishes and a pleasant setting. Also just off the square, at the south end near the cinema, '**Eikosipend-eráki**' serves good *mezés* and has live *rebetiko* music on occasions. Lastly, at the east end of the harbour on Kanaris Square, '**Ta Giannena**' may look dowdy but it has fresh and well-prepared traditional dishes, with good service; it represents a type of mid-20th century traditional Greek-city-restaurant which is fast disappearing in the islands.

GLOSSARY OF CLASSICAL, BYZANTINE & GREEK TERMS

agora—a large public space, mainly given over to commerce

Archaic period—the 7th and 6th centuries BC

ashlar—stone masonry using large, dressed, regular blocks

bouzouki—a large, oriental mandolin with a distinctive, shimmering tone

Cabiri—divinities associated with 'Mystery' sanctuaries, esp. Samothrace

catholicon—the church at the centre of an Orthodox monastery

chlamys—a simple, versatile, woollen cloak or cape used in the ancient world, worn in several different ways by Greek men, either on its own or over other clothing, and most frequently pinned at the shoulder.

cloisonné—(in masonry) the 'framing' or separating of cut blocks of stone with thin ceramic tiles in the construction of a wall

depas **cup**—(a term taken from Homer) a tall, footless cup with two elongated handles *dromos*—an entrance passage or axial approach to a tomb or building

epitaphios—the image of the dead Christ, richly embroidered in textile, carried in the Easter Saturday procession

Geometric period—the 10th-late 8th centuries BC

Hellenistic period—era of, and after, the campaigns of Alexander the Great, c. 330–c.150 BC

iconostasis—the high wooden screen (generally holding icons and images) which separates the sanctuary from the main body of an Orthodox church and which with time came to substitute the masonry templon (*see below*) of earlier Byzantine churches

isodomic—(of masonry) constructed in parallel courses of neatly-cut rectangular blocks

Iznik—the Turkish name for ancient Nicaea; in the 16th and 17th centuries especially, it was the sole source of a fine, glazed ceramic ware with very particular colours which has generically been given the name 'Iznik ware'

kore—the statue of a robed, standing female figure, common in Archaic sculpture (*cp kouros below*)

kouros—the statue of a nude, male figure, common in Archaic sculpture

machicolation—a defensive projection out from a fortified building, often over the entrance or at a corner,

from which projectiles or hot liquids could be dropped
on assailants

naos—the central interior area of a Byzantine church or
the inside chamber of a pagan temple

nymphaeum—a place (often by a spring, or in a grotto,
or underground) consecrated to the worship of the
nymphs—divinities of springs and fresh water

pithos (pl. *pithoi*)—a large, tall, ceramic storage jar,
sometimes used also for burials

pronaos—the front vestibule of a temple, preceding the
naos

prytaneion—the 'town-hall' or office of the chief(s) of
an ancient city

pyxis—a (generally) cylindrical vessel with a lid, often
used in Antiquity by women as a box for containing
cosmetics

rebetiko (pl. *rebetika*)—the often plangent and nostalgic
song-tradition of the Greek refugees from Asia Minor
which first became widely popular in the 1960s and 70s

spolia—elements and fragments from ancient buildings
re-used in later constructions

stele (pl. *stelai*,)—a carved tablet or grave-stone

stoa—a long, covered colonnade open on one side and
closed (by shops or offices) on the other

templon—the stone or masonry screen in a church

which closes off the sanctuary

thesmophoreion—a place for the ritual worship of Demeter, mostly frequented by women

INDEX

General

General continued

Nigel McGilchrist is an art historian who has lived in the Mediterranean—Italy, Greece and Turkey—for over 30 years, working for a period for the Italian Ministry of Arts and then for six years as Director of the Anglo-Italian Institute in Rome. He has taught at the University of Rome, for the University of Massachusetts, and was for seven years Dean of European Studies for a consortium of American universities. He lectures widely in art and archaeology at museums and institutions in Europe and the United States, and lives near Orvieto.